BIRD CARDS

As kingfishers catch fire, dragonflies draw flame;
As tumbled over rim in roundy wells
Stones ring; like each tucked string tells, each hung bell's
Bow swung finds tongue to fling out broad its name;
Each mortal thing does one thing and the same:
Deals out that being indoors each one dwells;
Selves – goes itself; myself it speaks and spells,
Crying What I do is me: for that I came.

I say more: the just man justices;
Keeps grace: that keeps all his goings graces;
Acts in God's eye what in God's eye he is –
Christ. For Christ plays in ten thousand places,
Lovely in limbs and lovely in eyes not his
To the Father through the features of men's faces.

Gerard Manley Hopkins, 1882

Jane Toerien

Bird Cards

The Healing Power
of the Bird Kingdom

Illustrated by Joyce van Dobben

Altamira-Becht · Haarlem

© 2007 Published by Uitgeverij Altamira-Becht BV, Postbus 317, 2000 AH Haarlem,
the Netherlands
(e-mail: post@gottmer.nl)
Uitgeverij Altamira-Becht BV is part of the Gottmer Publishing Group BV, Haarlem,
the Netherlands

Cover design: Marius Brouwer, Haarlem
Photography: Martijn Zegel
Typesetting: Peter Verwey Grafische Produkties bv, Heemstede

ISBN 978 90 6963 748 8

www.altamira-becht.nl
www.diepmagazine.nl

Contents

Foreword

As an author myself, I enjoy the conception, gestation, and finally the birthing of my books; yes, I really do see it like that! There is an holistic process involved, energy that is working on levels similar to those of the human birthing process. Seldom, however, do I ever get to participate in this process with another author. Certainly I was absent at the conception! That happened for Jane, no doubt, in a quiet moment of inspiration, probably followed by an easy gestation… then came the birthing. This was not so easy. There were painful moments of slow pushing, moments when the new baby couldn't come quickly enough, and periods of long waiting as the new baby chose its timing to emerge into the presence of humanity.

During all this, I gave the sort of encouragement any birthing receives, murmuring words of support, of praise and the occasional words of advice. Now, as the newborn Bird Cards and Book are being clothed in their garments of manifestation, I am happy to act as a kind of midwife, offering sincere and positive words to ease them into the world.

What a wonderful partnership we have in this presentation. First there was Jane, with her ability to cross the membrane between the physical and metaphysical expressions of bird consciousness; and then came Joyce, with her ability to attune with, and perceive, the bird consciousness, expressing this with her beautiful, descriptive pictures. I want you, the reader, to know just how rare this is. Two people attuned to the same vision, the same purpose, the same intent, both synchronised together into a seamless Whole.

As some of you may know, Nature was/is my teacher. I have the ability to 'listen' to the silent words that flow from Nature. This is a simple process, but not easy. Listeners are required to close down all their own concepts, ideas, beliefs, expectations, and knowledge about Nature, enabling themselves to become purely receptive and responsive. Too often the listener's own agenda gets in the way, such as fears and worries about world events, or anger at perceived ecological destruction. If a person believes that humanity or Nature must be 'saved', and has a desire to 'help' in this process, then the ability to 'listen' is so diluted as it filters through desires and concepts that the resulting words are no more than an echo of the listener's beliefs. Jane fell into none of these traps. She listened. She was enthralled, enthusiastic, excited, bewildered, and happy, and she had no idea initially where it was all leading to, or why.

Joyce came into the picture – literally! – in perfect timing. Her current project had just finished, and she and Jane were put in touch with each other by a friend. Although during the whole time Joyce envisioned and created the cards they had yet to meet physically, they certainly met and connected on the required level of consciousness.

Just as I had been inspired and, frankly, surprised by the quality and insight of Jane's words, so I was powerfully impressed by the quality of Joyce's visual interpretation of each expression of bird energy. Again, I cannot help but emphasise that this is a rare combination. Both Jane and Joyce have put aside their personality packages and have attuned on a high and distinctly clear level of communication with both the Book and the Cards. Both the words and the pictures are inspirations of communication. Communication comes on many levels; it can be intellectual, boring, aggressive, demanding… the list is long, but really to connect, communication needs to involve the heart. Long after the head has forgotten, the heart remembers – and acts. This is the class and this the quality of the Bird Cards and Book communication: as a package they are definitely heart quality, heart expression.

I thoroughly recommend the Bird Cards and Book, and I suggest that you use them with receptivity and openness, allowing your own inner response to emerge. Don't so much 'do' with them, rather… 'be' with them!

Michael J Roads,
Author: *Talking With Nature, Journey into Nature, Journey into Oneness, Into a Timeless Realm, and The Magic Formula.*

Introduction

The process of bringing these Bird Cards to birth has been its own soul journey, full of mystery and deep meaning for both myself and my companion along the road, Joyce van Dobben, who brought the text to life with her exquisite pictures.

It began just after New Year, 1999, in Cape Town, South Africa. At the time I was doing counselling work with people, helping them to access and clear deep emotional issues, and in the process I often used oracular card sets as a fun process to help reflect back to the person what the issues might be. I also enjoyed using flower essences for myself, as a gentle vibrational healing tool to cleanse and heal the emotional body. I have always felt very connected to birds, and I had been playing with the thought that if flowers offer vibrational healing to the world, maybe in some way birds are offering healing too.

That particular evening, I settled down for a meditation and found myself drawn into a very deep still space inside myself. From this still place, my inner voice spoke clearly to me. I was reminded of this thought I had been having, and told to 'just sit down and write and see what happens'. I did so, and to my astonishment, out came 'the Pigeon'. None of it was information I knew consciously. It was not that my hand wrote automatically, or that I felt taken over by someone else, I was writing it myself – but I stayed in that still place, and from that place came an authority and wisdom I did not know I had. Over the next year I would repeatedly feel myself being drawn into that place, until all 55 birds had emerged.

In the process, I was put through a soul journey of my own. Each of the issues the birds represent became my issue, and until I had dealt with it sufficiently, I was not able to move on, sometimes being stuck on one paragraph for up to a month. I never knew which bird I was going to write next until I sat down to write the heading, nor did I have any idea where it was going to stop, until I wrote 'the Blue Bird of Happiness', and realised that this was the essence of it all, and there was no need to go further. It was interesting to me to find out later that in the Aura-Soma system of colour-healing, where the numbers of each coloured bottle have deep esoteric significance, bottle number 55 is the number of the Christ.

Michael Roads has been kind enough to write the foreword to this book, which is appropriate, as he and his wife, Treenie, have really been the major catalysts for its birth. In 1994 my husband and I had read his book 'Journey into Nature' (published by H. J. Kramer Inc, Tiburon, California, 1990), which is his own personal story of his metaphysical relationship with nature, and how through his experience of the Oneness of all life, he awakened to his own Self. We were so inspired by this story that we flew to America to attend a week-long workshop, and subsequently invited them to South Africa to give workshops on Self-realization – and became friends in the process. To quote from 'the Blue Bird of Happiness': 'We are all One. You are a part of me. I come to you as a part of your Self, bringing the reminder that the essence of who you are is God. You are a magnificent being made in the image of God. You experience yourself as separate from God, but we are like the angels – we know that there is no separation and that God simply is in us. Our presence in your lives is God's blessing to this planet, to keep the possibility of joy and love and peace alive here, until you realise that you *are* it.'

This is nature-mysticism; the knowing that God is omnipresent, and therefore we are all connected in that, and that through nature we can encounter both God and Self, because it is all One.

During the course of the year in which I was writing the Bird Cards, I went to Austria to attend an international gathering of people who had attended retreats of Michael and Treenie Roads. Here I must acknowledge Siska Pothof, who, after hearing what I was doing, told me about her friend Joyce van Dobben, from Holland, who was a bird enthusiast, a spiritual artist, and who was looking for a new uplifting project for her art. As she told me about Joyce a huge thunderstorm broke loose, with thunder, lightning and hailstones. Just in case I didn't get the message, nature was saying 'YES!'

I was delighted with the samples of cards that Joyce produced, and the fact that she was also completely familiar with the philosophy the Bird Cards are expressing, and we proceeded to communicate across the continents by e-mail. Joyce began a similar process to my own in the sense of needing to be in a still space to access the inspirational ideas that came to her, and also having to move through the issues the bird energies represented in her own life, often getting stuck for a while on a particular bird until she had got the point. I love the symbols and gemstones that she has intuitively chosen for each bird, they always felt just right when I saw them for the first time. She describes how she was at a concert one evening, when the whole concept of the Phoenix card, with the puzzle-pieces falling away to reveal a new reality, popped into her head. The process of the illustration of the cards took three years, and although we had never met we became great friends, so that when we did finally meet in September 2002 we were old companions already.

While Joyce was doing the drawings of the Bird Cards, another extraordinary process was unfolding for me. In August 1999 there was a solar eclipse that astrologers felt was an important event in the unfolding consciousness of humanity. Over this period, my inner voice instructed me to prepare 55 bottles of pure spring water. Over the period of the eclipse I had to hold each of them in turn, and the 'overlighting consciousness' of each bird described in the Bird Cards, fused its energy to the water, thus creating a 'bird essence', each bird essence offering harmonising for the specific issues that the bird represents. On December 4th 2002, there was another important solar eclipse, which was apparently a completion of a cycle begun in August 1999, and again I had to hold each essence as the bird consciousness fused with it, and this time was told that the essences were now being completed and sealed. These essences will be available eventually as gentle harmonising tools to assist people to align with their true Selves. (For those who are interested, the website for the essences is www. birdcards.co.za).

The term 'overlighting consciousness' that has been used in this book, really is synonymous with the term 'deva', or 'angel'. Each species of bird, flower, tree, and other forms of nature, has an organising force behind it that is intelligent and connected to the greater whole, which is God. I felt the reality of this intelligence, the power and beauty of it, and its connection to the whole, when I was making the essences, so I know that when the affirmations suggest that you 'ask the overlighting consciousness of this bird to help you', you are drawing a real and active assisting energy into your life, and it is not make-believe. It is also entirely beneficent and good – it is part of God.

There were two incidents that I suppose could be seen now as foreshadowings of this connection with the bird kingdom. The first occurred in 1994; my husband and I had just bought a plot of land in a lovely green valley overlooking a lake, and were walking onto the property with a dear friend, to admire the view, and start the process of deciding where we should best build our house. As a young girl I had been a great bird-watcher, and spent hours at our family holiday house sitting as quietly as I could in the bushes, hoping that a bird might come and eat from my hand, or sit on my shoulder. To my disappointment, it never happened. Now, as we walked onto the hill where our future house would be built, I saw to my astonishment that there was a little brightly-coloured bird on the ground. It was a swee waxbill, usually a very lively little bird. I thought it must be hurt, so I bent down next to it and put my hand out gently. It climbed into the palm of my hand, and nestled there, completely trusting, for quite a few minutes, while I hardly breathed. The overwhelming energy that I received from its little body was this message of 'trust'. Then it quite perkily shook its feathers, chirped at me, and flew away. The house was built, and in fact quite a few of the Bird Cards were written on its verandah a few years later.

The other incident was a dream that I had shortly after meeting Michael and Treenie Roads for the first time, also in 1994. In the dream I was sitting with them at a restaurant table. I was showing them a book that it appeared I had written; the title on the front of the book was 'As Kingfishers Catch Fire' (the first line of one of my favourite Gerard Manley Hopkins poems). Michael smiled at me, and said 'It's kingfisher time'. I had no idea what this meant for many years, but the memory of the dream stayed with me clearly. I understood better when I wrote the Bird Cards, of course, but the recognition went even further when Joyce sent me the first sample of her work, and she had chosen the Kingfisher!

I have used these Bird Cards very successfully as a help in my counselling of other people – at the end of a session for example, I might ask the person to draw a card and read the message out loud to me. Often it has been so apt as to make grown men cry! One can use them in many ways for oneself; I like to pick a card daily, just to sense the kind of energy the day offers and the lessons that are uppermost at the time. I also often have significant encounters with birds in my daily life, and then I am amazed at the accuracy of the message, when I read the card. For example, just before Joyce, the artist, was to arrive in Cape Town to meet me for the first time, my car was flagged down by my neighbour who wanted me to slow down in the road, because there walking solemnly across the road were a mother goose and seven goslings, with father goose bringing up the rear! Not something I have ever seen before in our suburbs. Goose energy is about triumph and completion – I loved that message. And similarly, when I arrived at Joyce's house in Holland for the first time, a magnificent pheasant was there to greet me, the message to both of us being that we must love and acknowledge ourselves for this project. This is what I love about having the Bird Cards in my life – it enables life to talk back to me with its own special symbols. In the chapter on 'Ways to Use the Cards', I have described some more specific ways in which you can play with the cards to get insights about your life.

It is clear, through the gift of the Bird Cards, and also my experience of making the essences, that the bird kingdom is wishing to connect with us, and to offer us its very specific and powerful help at this crucial time in the planet's history. Through the Bird Cards, the bird kingdom is alerting us to the fact that it is there for a purpose, and can be called upon; we only have to ask.

Jane Toerien

The Artist's Story

Two weeks after I had sent out a request to life for a new and uplifting spiritual art project, I was put in touch with Jane, as described in her Introduction, and a very rich and wondrous creative process started for me.

The sequence in which I drew the cards was different from the sequence in which Jane wrote them. I just listened to the inner impulse of which bird was making itself 'known' to me, and the sequence in which they came was part of my own individual 'birth process'. The symbols I chose for the backgrounds often came to me at the most unexpected moments. I would make notes of them when they came to me, because often I did not know yet how or where I would use them. I have given detailed explanations of my choice of symbols in the Artist's Notes, at the end of the book.

For example, it has been described in the Introduction how the idea for 'the Phoenix' card, of the puzzle-pieces of the old reality falling away to reveal a new world, came into my head during a pause in a concert that a dear friend had invited me to attend with her. At the time, I did not know which bird this symbol was referring to.

Often the bird I was drawing appeared to be synchronously connected with events that were unfolding in my own life, or even with world events. I had almost completed 'the Roller' when, on September 11, 2001, the twin towers of the World Trade Centre in New York collapsed. It felt to me as if the bird energy was offering the possibility of 'waking up' to our true Selves, beyond separation, through this synchronicity. And the bird that felt appropriate to draw after that was 'the Cuckoo', signalling the start of a new cycle.

To illustrate the background of the bird, I chose from the text a fragment, or concept, to which I felt able to give symbolic form. 'The Lovebird' process was a particularly remarkable one; the text speaks about how the lovebird energy expresses Archangel Michael's divinely inspired mission on this planet, to hold a forcefield of love to help lift up each creature and element upon this earth. In the process of drawing the heart in the sky, a silhouetted figure of Archangel Michael appeared within it; not my doing at all, in fact I have not included a 'human' form in any of the drawings.

As Jane describes for herself, I was sometimes stuck on one particular bird for a long time. I redid 'the Hummingbird' five times and was still not satisfied. I then had the impulse to do 'the Vulture'; this came quite easily, and once I had finished it, I found that 'the Hummingbird' fell into place as well.

I chose intuitively the gems and minerals that I used in the drawings, it had to feel 'right'. For 'the Dodo', for example, I felt very strongly that I should use snowflake obsidian, which is a volcanic mineral – and subsequently discovered that the dodo had existed only on two volcanic islands, which was something I had not known before.

I am so grateful to have been involved in this unique project!

Joyce van Dobben

Ways to Use the Cards

'Have fun now, and enjoy the nectar of life'
('the Sunbird')

As I described in the Introduction, the Bird Cards have really become a way of life for me; they have taught me how to see the world in a new way, as an extension of my Self, mirroring back to me messages and affirmations, that make me feel so much more loved, supported, and connected to the whole of life.

The most obvious and immediate way to use the Bird Cards is simply to shuffle the pack, spread the cards and pick one, then read the message in the text. The message will mirror back to you the energy that you are expressing in that moment. You can also hold a question in your mind, and pick a card, and the card will throw some light on the question you are asking. In this chapter, the section 'Working with the Affirmations', will explain the full implication of saying the affirmation at the end of the text, once you have read your chosen card.

There is no such thing as a 'reversed card' in this system. It is a good idea to turn all the cards the right way up to begin with, but if one happens to be upside-down, just read the text as usual.

The cards can be used in a therapy practice, as an aid, to bring an uplifting and timely message to the person involved. Here, in most cases, the person will simply choose a card from the shuffled pack, and read the message – but a therapist who is familiar with the spreads given further on, could also incorporate these into the therapy process, as they can be very revealing.

If you have a special encounter with a bird, either in real life, or in a dream or a meditation, the book can be there as a reference, to help you decipher the metaphor and the message. Sometimes people feel that they have a 'special bird', or their own bird symbol, then it is very revealing to read about this in the text. In this chapter is a spread that can help you determine your own bird symbol.

I use the cards as a daily reading, to give me a sense of the energy I need to work with during the day. In the writing of the cards, I felt as if I was being put through a profound mystery school, where I encountered the energy of each bird in turn, and had to work with it until I had completed that lesson, and then could move on to the next bird. This is another way you can use the Bird Cards for yourself – the numbers are not arbitrary, and the sequence is there for a reason; you can put yourself through your own mystery school process by encountering the energy and lessons of each bird, and using the affirmations, one by one. You will find your own way of knowing when it is time to move forward, or whether you need to follow your own individual sequence – for example, you could use a pendulum, or muscle-testing, if you are familiar with these methods. If you have a deep commitment to your own Self-realization, you will find this a very rewarding and profound process.

Overlighting conciousness and God

You will notice when you read the text that it refers often to the 'overlighting consciousness' of each bird. The overlighting consciousness of the bird is the 'deva', or 'angel' of the bird. This term has been chosen because it conveys the sense of the 'umbrella' of consciousness that contains each group of birds within itself. By 'group' of birds, I mean those birds which can be recognised as having similar qualities, such as sparrow-type birds, hawk-type birds, partridge-type birds, and so on. Each overlighting consciousness is an intelligent, invisible, organising force. When you have read some of the birds in the text, you will see that each one offers a different kind of healing energy. The significant appearance of a bird in your life, either in actuality or by choosing a Bird Card, or in a meditation or dream, alerts you to the fact that this greater consciousness, of which the bird is an expression, is calling your attention, because its energy can assist with your current situation.

Because nothing is separate in the realm of consciousness (we are all actually One vast, intelligent consciousness), you are never truly alone. The metaphysical world, of which these overlighting consciousnesses are a part, is always connected and aware of everything that is happening, both in you and in everything in the universe.

Overlighting all the individual bird consciousnesses is the overlighting consciousness of the bird kingdom, a being of enormous compassion and joy, closely connected to the Archangel Raphael, who is in charge of the realm of healing. And overlighting all the Archangels and everything else, is Spirit, also known as God, which is omnipresent, and therefore in every particle of matter in the universe.

I have chosen the word 'God', as opposed to 'Spirit', in the text, because I like the more personal feel of it. I certainly do not envisage God as a Father Christmas-type figure sitting on a cloud, dispensing rather arbitrary blessings or punishments upon me. But I do experience God as both intensely personal, and vastly impersonal. God is everything there is, but this implies that God is also you and me. The God that is me, I call Self, and discovering the Divinity of Self is what Self-realisation is all about. A Self-realised person experiences him or herself as One with God, and therefore with the Universe. This is actually the path we are all treading, whether we realise it or not – the path back to the re-remembering that each of us is, in essence, God. We have never been other than God, we have simply chosen to have an experience of forgetting. We have been asleep, and it is only by choosing to remember that we will wake up.

This is where the affirmations in this book come in; they give us the choice to ask for help. We have free will here – we have the free will to choose to stay asleep by not asking for help. Or, we can choose to ask for help. Saying the affirmations is one way of asking, and the response will be real, bringing the healing energy of the bird kingdom, which is in itself a gift of God.

Working with the affirmations

When you do the spreads, or simply choose one card, you are being given the opportunity to invite an active assistance into your life, to help with your issues, in the form of the overlighting consciousness of each bird (see the previous section on 'Overlighting Consciousness and God'). However, to engage this assistance you have to actually ask (not merely read the text). You ask by saying the given affirmation aloud, or simply by asking in your own words for help.

As soon as you ask for help, the energy of the bird will be present for you in your energy field, but, this is important: *if you are working with an issue over a period of time, you must repeat the affirmation daily to re-energise the bird energy in your life.* If you only say it once, and then forget about it, there will be an immediate response, and you will feel a shift within you, but the connection will fade over time.

Saying the affirmation daily also reminds you of what you are working with, so that you are keeping it conscious for yourself at the same time. It is a good idea to write the affirmation on a piece of paper, cut it out and paste it somewhere such as your bathroom mirror, so that you are reminded to restate it often.

Clarity of intent

In the instructions for the spreads on the next few pages, I have repeatedly suggested that you decide which of the spreads you wish to use, and then *state this clearly in your mind, or out loud, or write it down.* Preferably all three. This is because life responds best to a very clear and focused intent. Focus and clarity of intent produce the clearest response in all situations you find yourself in, including choosing a Bird Card, or asking for clarification through a Bird Card spread. To get the best results from the spreads, it is necessary for you to be in an unhurried, relaxed frame of mind, with time to clarify your question and properly absorb the answer. Then you have honoured the process. You will get an answer, whatever state of mind you are in – sometimes the answer itself will help to clarify a confusion – but the clearer you are about the question, the more specific the answer will be.

The Spreads

The simplest way to use the Bird Cards is to shuffle the pack, fan the cards out, choose one and read the text. The bird that you choose will reflect back to you the energy that you are expressing in that moment. If you have a question, you can hold the question in your mind, and then choose a card, and the card will throw light upon that issue for you.

Apart from this simplest method of using the cards, there are seven spreads, which can be done in any order; the first two give you information about yourself as a soul, and these should each really only be done once. The remaining five are more to do with helping you get insight about issues that you are dealing with in your daily life, and they can be done as often as you like, depending on your need.

Sit comfortably with a flat surface in front of you on which to lay the cards. Have a notebook or journal handy to write down what happens, as the results often make more sense later. Decide which of the spreads you wish to use, *state this clearly in your mind, or out loud, or write it down*, then shuffle the cards. Sit quietly for a few moments, to centre yourself. When you feel ready, lay the cards out according to instruction.

'Special Bird' Spread

Choosing your own 'special bird' (1 card)

Many people already have a 'special bird', with which they feel a great affinity, and which appears for them often, either in real life or in dreams or meditations, or even as a recurring symbol in their artwork. In this case, it would be enough simply to read the relevant text. If you would like to know your own 'special bird', this spread will help you. The 'special bird' in your life is your 'heart bird' – it is the one that you resonate to very closely. Preferably do this spread only once; therefore do it at a time when you feel centred and are able to absorb the text and the affirmation fully.

You are going to lay out all the cards in the pack for this spread. You lay them out one by one, face-down, according to the design given. It doesn't matter what order you do this in, but complete the whole picture. As you can see, it forms the shape of a bird. The process of laying the cards out is in itself a kind of meditation, if you do it slowly and calmly. Once you have laid out the cards, look at the shape for a while. Don't be anxious about it, just take your time and allow your gaze to wander over the cards, letting your being settle down into a stillness. You will start to notice one particular card drawing your attention. There is no rush. Sit quietly until you are quite sure which one it is. Then turn it over and see which it is. Read the text, and then read the affirmation out loud. Refer to the section on 'Working With the Affirmations', to remind yourself how this works. You can use the affirmation of this bird on an ongoing basis, or just know that it is very close to your heart, and the essence of who you are.

'Special Bird'-spread

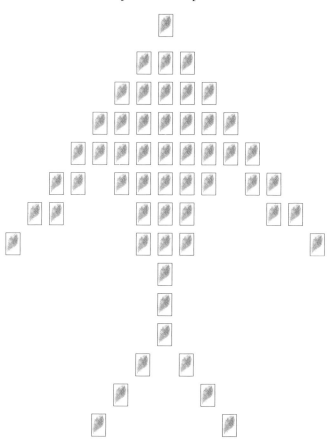

1 State clearly in your mind, or out loud, or write down, the fact that you are doing the 'Special Bird' Spread.
2 Shuffle the pack and then lay the cards face-down according to the pattern given here.
3 Sit quietly and feel which card is most drawing your attention.
4 When you are sure which it is, turn that card over to find your 'special bird'.
5 Read the explanation in the 'Special Bird' Spread, then read the text for the bird you have chosen.
6 Say the affirmation.
7 Write down what happened during this process.

Roller Spread

Reminding yourself who you are (2 cards)

In the depths of our being, we know who we are, the path that we have to follow to reach Self-realization, and the kind of work we do in the world. But for most of us, this is not information that is accessed very easily; we get glimpses now and again, but most of the time it is clouded over. This spread is a powerful one – it is designed to get you reacquainted with who you are, and what you do. Like the first spread, it should be done only once, and therefore at a time and in a place where you can really feel and absorb the information that comes to you. Write down the birds that appear for you, so that you can refer back to them often, to remind you who you are.

State clearly to yourself that you are going to do the Roller Spread now. Shuffle the pack well. When you feel ready, place the whole pack face-down on the flat surface. Now cut the pack into two portions. Put the top portion of the pack on the right-hand side of the lower portion, and turn over the top card of the lower portion. This is Card 1 in the illustration.

The card you have turned over represents *the path that you need to follow to achieve Self-realisation*. Everyone is different, and each person is following a very different path to the same goal. What is your individual path? This card is giving you the answer. Read the text and absorb what this means for you. Write the name of the bird down, together with your thoughts and feelings about this, so that you can refer to it again. Say the affirmation out loud, and write this down too. Refer to the section on 'Working With the Affirmations', to remind yourself about the power of this.

When you are ready to move on, take the upper portion of the pack (the one that you put on the right-hand side), and cut this into two more portions, again putting the new upper portion on the right-hand side. Turn over the top card on the new lower portion. This is Card 2 in the illustration.

The card you have turned over represents *the work you do in the world.*
This has very likely no resemblance to your daily job. It is referring to
the impact you have, because of who you are. Take time to absorb the
meaning of this card for you. Read the text, and write down the bird,
and your thoughts and feelings about this. Say the affirmation, write it
down and refer to it often.

Now the clouds have parted for a moment, and the light has shone
through. It is up to you what you do with this moment of revelation
about who you are and what you can do. If you keep re-energising
this revelation by stating the affirmations daily, you will find that what
you have found out about yourself is no longer clouded, but a clear
expression of who you are.

Roller Spread

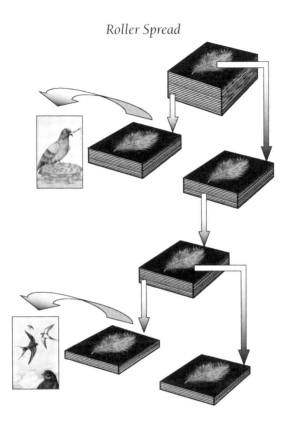

1 Shuffle and split the full pack
2 Place the top portion on the right
3 Place the bottom portion on the left
4 Turn over top card of bottom portion
Card 1
5 Split the right hand pile
6 Place the top portion on the right
7 Place the bottom portion on the left
8 Turn over top card of bottom portion
Card 2
9 Read the explanation in the Roller Spread to see what Card 1 and 2
   represent, and read the text for each bird you have chosen.
10 Say each affirmation.
11 Write down what happened during this process.

Swallow Spread

Expanding the self (6 cards)

Hold your shuffled pack of cards, and fan them out face-down on the flat surface in front of you. State clearly in your mind that you are going to do the Swallow Spread, for expanding the self, and then choose one card. *The card you choose first will represent you as you are now.* This is Card 1 in the illustration. Turn it face-up in front of you and read the text. Take time to absorb the implications of what you are reading, and perhaps write down your thoughts about your choice.

Next, choose 5 more cards from the fanned-out pack, and arrange them around the first one, face-down. *They represent attributes that you need to focus on and develop, in order to express your full potential.* It doesn't matter in which order you read these, but in each case, take time to absorb what the card is saying, (preferably writing your thoughts down, so that you can refer to the process again at a later date), and then say the affirmation for that card, thus consciously inviting each of these 5 bird energies to be in your life, helping you to grow. Reread the section on 'Working With the Affirmations', to remind yourself how to do this. As explained in that section, you will have to re-energise each affirmation every day to keep that assistance active and working in your life, so that there is progress. It will be interesting for you to read this again in a few months' time, and to see how you have moved forward with these issues.

Swallow Spread

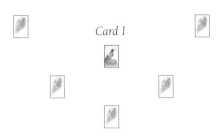

Card 1

1 State clearly in your mind, or out loud, or write down, the fact that you are going to do the Swallow Spread for expanding the self.
2 Choose one card from the shuffled and fanned-out pack. This is Card 1.
3 Read the explanation in the Swallow Spread to see what this card represents, and read the text for the bird you have chosen.
4 Choose five more cards, and place them face-down in any order around Card 1.
5 Read the explanation in the Swallow Spread to see what these cards represent, then turn them over and read the text of each bird you have chosen.
6 Say each affirmation.
7 Write down what happened during this process.
8 Repeat each affirmation daily to keep the energy active in your life to help you to express your full potential.

Stork Spread

Achieving a goal (7 cards)

This is the spread to use when there is a particular state of being, or goal, you wish to achieve. The process will help you to see what is blocking the attainment of that goal in different areas of your life. To do this properly, you need to give yourself a lot of time, because there will be much to absorb and think about.

Think about the goal you wish to work with, state it out loud, or write it down. Hold the shuffled pack of cards, fan them out face-down on your flat surface, choose a card, and lay it face-up in front of you. (This is Card 1 in the illustration.) This card is *the bird that you have chosen to represent your goal*. Once you know what the bird is, read the text in the book that describes the card you have chosen. Think about what you have read for a while, to understand why it might have appeared for you to describe your goal. It might be useful to write down your thoughts in your journal or notebook.

The next 6 cards in the spread are going to represent *different areas of your life which need to be addressed in order to achieve this state of being, or goal, described by Card 1*. Now pick 6 cards (Cards 2 to 7) from the fanned-out pack, and lay them in the order you have chosen them, face-down, in a line separate from Card 1. You are going to turn them over one by one, and I will describe what they represent.

I suggest that you write your thoughts down, and say the affirmation aloud after reading each text, before moving on to the next card. It is a good idea to read the section on 'Working With the Affirmations' at this point, before you proceed.

CARD 2: *family*. The bird you have chosen is the energy you need to work with to clear issues to do with family, to help you to come closer to the goal described in Card 1. Once you have absorbed the unique meaning of the card for your life (you may have to read it a few times to get the point of how it is relevant for you specifically), say the affirmation out loud and move on to the next card.

CARD 3: *partnership*. The bird you have chosen is the energy you need to work with to move forward with significant partnerships in your life, so that there is nothing in this area that might be blocking the fulfilment of your goal.

CARD 4: *your work in the world*. The bird you have chosen is the energy you need to be aware of in relation to your work in the world, to enhance the attainment of your goal. Your 'work in the world' is either your actual job, or what you potentially could offer as a service, or just who you are and the effect you have on others by being here.

CARD 5: *your self-esteem*. Everyone needs help with this issue, and the bird that you choose will be the specific one that will most help you gain confidence, so that you can grow towards your goal.

CARD 6: *the area in which you need to make progress spiritually*. Again, the bird that you choose will be the one whose energy will be right to help you make a breakthrough spiritually, as part of the movement towards your goal.

CARD 7: *your greatest asset, that you can harness to help achieve the goal*. You might be surprised at what life shows you here – sometimes we do not see our greatest strengths for the assets they are. Whatever comes to you here – really hear it and let it in!

Stork Spread

Card 1

2   3   4   5   6   7

1 Think about the goal you wish to work with, state it out loud, or write it down.
2 Shuffle the cards, fan them out face-down and choose a card.
3 Lay it face-up in front of you. This is card 1.
4 Read the explanation of the storkspread to find out what card 1 means and read the text in the book that describes the card you have chosen.
5 Now pick 6 cards (Cards 2 to 7) from the fanned-out pack, and lay them in the order you have chosen them, face-down, in a line separate from Card 1.
6 Read in each case the explanation of the storkspread to see what the position of the card means, turn it over and read the text that describes the card you have chosen.
7 Say, after reading each text, the affirmation that goes with it.
8 Write down what happens to you.
9 Repeat each affirmation dayly, or at least the affirmation that is most important to you, to keep the energy in your life active and to help you to achieve your goal.

Cormorant Spread

Resolving a problem (3 cards)

This is the spread to use when there is an issue or intractable problem
that you are struggling with. Focus on your problem first, say it out
loud, or write it down, and then ask for the most appropriate help.
When you feel centred, fan out the shuffled pack face-down on your
flat surface, and choose 3 cards. Lay the 3 cards out face-down in a line,
in the order in which you choose them. As you turn over each one and
read the text, it will be very helpful to write your thoughts down before
you move on to the next card.

CARD 1: *the core issue at the root of the problem.* The bird that you choose
will give you the picture of what the main issue is here – perhaps there
is a lack of forgiveness, or a lack of self-love, or an inability to let go. You
will have to interpret the card according to the specific circumstances of
the problem.

CARD 2: *the specific energy that you need to call on to move the process
forward.* This is the bird that is offering itself to you in the current
circumstances, to help you to resolve the issue at hand. It is important
that you say the affirmation here, and actively invite this bird energy
into your life, to help. Write the affirmation down and place this
somewhere in your environment where you will see it and can reaffirm
it often, to remind you that you have this help in your life. (Read the
section on 'Working With the Affirmations', to remind yourself how this
works).

CARD 3: *the energy that will be released once the problem is resolved.* The
bird that is chosen here gives you a picture of what life might feel like,
once this whole issue moves forward – it is something to look forward
to, so to speak. Write it down so that you can remind yourself of what
you are moving towards.

Cormorant Spread

1   2   3

1 Focus on your problem, state it out loud, or write it down, then ask for the most appropriate help.
2 Choose three cards from the shuffled and fanned-out pack.
3 Lay them face-down in a row from left to right in the order they were chosen (Cards 1 to 3).
4 Turn them over one at a time, in that order. Read the explanation in the Cormorant Spread to see what each placing represents, then read the text for each bird you have chosen.
5 Say the affirmations for each bird, especially the bird chosen for Card 2.
6 Write down what happened during this process.
7 Write down and cut out the affirmation for the bird you have chosen for Card 2, and put it up somewhere where you will see it and repeat it often, to help you to resolve your problem.

Nightjar Spread

Dealing with a fear (4 cards)

This is the spread you will use when you need help to clear a constantly recurring worry, or to give you strength if something is looming. In this case, you will focus on the fear you need help with, say it out loud, or write it down. Then ask that the appropriate help might be offered you. When you feel centred, hold the shuffled pack and fan it out face-down onto your flat surface. Now choose 4 cards from the pack and place them face-down in a line in front of you. *Each of these cards represents a bird that has been chosen to help you with your fear*. Turn over each one with a spirit of gratitude. Read the texts of each of the four birds, say the affirmations and thank the birds involved for being with you at this time to give you strength. Write them down, with your thoughts about why they might have been chosen for you, so that you can remind yourself that they are there. Read the section on 'Working With the Affirmations'. Over the next few days, repeatedly reaffirm their presence in your life, and notice how things feel lighter and easier.

Nightjar Spread

1 Focus on the fear you need help with, say it out loud, or write it down, then ask for the most appropriate help.
2 Choose four cards from the shuffled and fanned-out pack.
3 Lay them face-down.
4 Read the explanation in the Nightjar Spread to see what all four cards represent.
5 Turn them over one by one in any order.
6 Read the text of each bird you have chosen.
7 Say each affirmation, and thank each bird for being with you at this time to give you strength.
8 Write down what happened during this process.
9 Repeat each affirmation daily to keep the energy active in your life to help you to deal with your fear.

Pheasant Spread

Your strengths and undiscovered potential (5 cards)

Rather than focusing on a problem, this spread wants to show you your best assets. Hold the shuffled pack, and fan it out face-down on your flat surface. Choose the first one, Card 1 in the illustration, and place it face-up in front of you. Now choose two cards, Cards 2 and 3, and place them face-down on the left of Card 1. Then choose two more cards, Cards 4 and 5, and place them face-down on the right of Card 1. Now you can interpret the cards.

Card 1 represents *your undiscovered potential – that strength which you have within you, but which you have not yet tapped.* Read this card first, and write your thoughts down about it, before you turn over the others.

The two cards on the left, Cards 2 and 3, represent *the strengths that you came into this world with, that are already part of who you are as a soul.* The two cards on the right, Cards 4 and 5, represent *the new strengths that you have gained by being part of this world – the assets that you have acquired along the way this lifetime, as a result of your life-experiences.*

Take your time to read and absorb each one, writing down your thoughts as you go along – and really let in the affirmation of your strengths that life is giving you through these cards. These 4 assets (Cards 2, 3, 4 and 5) are the strengths that you can now harness in order to help your undiscovered potential (Card 1) to emerge into the light.

Read the affirmation from Card 1 out loud – you are asking the overlighting consciousness of the bird to help you to birth this unexpressed part of yourself. Read the section on 'Working With the Affirmations', to understand more about this.

Write all the cards down so that you can refer to them repeatedly and remind yourself of your strengths and what it is that you are trying to bring to birth for yourself. It is a good idea to write out the affirmation from Card 1 and put it on your bathroom mirror, or any place where you will notice it, to be stated as often as possible. This is an unconscious strength that you are trying to make conscious, and you need to be reminded that it is there, otherwise it will stay unrealised, and that would be a pity, because it is there, waiting to come out into the light.

Pheasant Spread

2   3   1   4   5

1   State clearly in your mind, or out loud, or write down, the fact that you are going to do the Pheasant Spread to show you your strengths and undiscovered potential.
2   Choose one card from the shuffled and fanned-out pack and lay it face-up. This is Card 1.
3   Read the explanation for what Card 1 represents in the Pheasant Spread, and then read the text for the bird you have chosen.
4   Say the affirmation.
5   Place two cards (Cards 2 and 3) face-down on the left of Card 1.
6   Place two cards (Cards 4 and 5) face-down on the right of Card 1.
7   Read the explanation in the Pheasant Spread to see what Cards 2, 3, 4 and 5 represent.
8   Turn them over one by one and read the text for each bird you have chosen.
9   Write down what happened in this process.
10 Write down the affirmation for the bird you have chosen for Card 1, cut it out and put it somewhere where you will see it and repeat it often. This keeps the energy active in your life to help your undiscovered potential to emerge into conscious awareness.

The Bird Cards

You are moving on the wings of Light to a new harmonic. We know about sound, and we know about flight. We can lift you up and help you to fly. These Bird Cards are given to you all to connect you with us, so that we can begin our task of moving you to this lighter expression of yourselves. We do things joyously, so this will be joyous too.

Each of you is beautiful beyond your present very limited conception of yourselves. We see the beauty in you; we know where you have come from and we know where you are going – come with us.

Do not ever get bogged down in fear and apprehension about this process of becoming a lighter version of yourself; just ask us to be there and we will. We know that it is a difficult challenge to be in a physical body. We can lift you up until you remember Who you are.

PIGEON

Affirmation

'I forgive with all my heart. I call upon the overlighting consciousness of the pigeon to transmute all negative energy from this situation and uplift it to a level where it expresses wholeness. I am whole. I see the wholeness in all things. I let go of all blame. I am free.'

Pigeon

The pigeon is the bird that is chosen for the first card because although it seems ordinary, it carries the message of forgiveness. Forgiveness transcends forever any residue of negativity that exists between warring opposites. It is the wholeness that comes once forgiveness is expressed that pigeon represents.

Do not take the pigeon for granted. Although it is represented in great numbers in places where people congregate, it is an important energy to have around. Flocks of pigeons stabilise earth energy in cities, allowing them to breathe more easily, and freeing trapped toxic energy that builds up in congested places. Bless the humble pigeon, you are truly privileged to have its presence in your life.

If you feel that the pigeon is your bird symbol, then know that your mission on earth is to mend what is broken. That life work can express itself in a myriad different ways, but each will carry the pigeon's promise of wholeness through the act of forgiveness.

When you draw the pigeon as part of a daily reading, or in answer to a question, then it is forgiveness that is being demanded of you within your particular situation. Pigeons may look for you if this is your issue – they love to zone in on a place that feels out of harmony.

Pigeon energy provides loving assistance to anyone undergoing a process of coming to the point of being able to forgive someone or something. Invite the pigeon into your process and meditations, and profound positive shifts will take place. Polluted places can be cleansed by asking the overlighting consciousness of the pigeon to uplift and transmute the pollution. Any unhappy situation can be uplifted in the same way.

You energise your planet by using the energy of the pigeon in this way. Your future depends on a partnership with nature. Using the wonderful gifts of the bird kingdom is partnering nature in a way which will have permanent impact on the toxicity levels of the planet.

2　　**SWALLOW**　　**2**

Affirmation

'I now align myself with my own personal path to joy. I invite the overlighting consciousness of the swallow to assist me to remove all blockages in the way of this alignment. I permit joy to enter my life. I place myself completely in the flow of my own natural rhythm and trust that in my own perfect timing I will experience joy.'

Swallow

The swallow brings the mystery of perfect alignment with one's joy. The swallow knows its joy, and follows it absolutely. Although it takes enormous effort to get where it has to be, the swallow presses on regardless. It knows that the journey's end will be worth it.

Every single person has programmed within him or her a map of how to get to that ultimate joy. The swallow energy provides a boost to help you to connect with that map and use it purposefully.

Finding one's joy is a process. Everyone makes mistakes and learns from them what is not one's joy. The ultimate joy is always that which brings you back to your Self. It is the path that leads you to the fullest expression of who you really are. Once you are expressing that in your life you are perfectly aligned with your joy.

Every person struggles to find the right expression of themselves. Many paths are chosen and some are better than others. Through the choosing, one slowly learns better and better what leads to joy and what doesn't.

Your card is saying to you that joy exists in your life. You are perhaps feeling that fate is handing you bitter blows, and cannot see that life could hold any joy for you. The message of the swallow for you today is that joy will come. It may be a long hard journey, but if you find your own inner map it will take you unerringly to a place where joy exists within you. Everyone has that place, and everyone has his or her own map.

People who feel particularly identified with the swallow as their symbol are progressing along their paths towards joy with a sense of purpose. They know where they are going and have a pretty good idea of how to get there. Their choices have become powerfully attuned to their end goal. They are usually spiritual seekers. Their joy is ultimate union with the Divine. In the process, they learn better and better how to express their own individual personalities in ways which allow full range of all their potential. To be expressing one's full potential is one's greatest joy.

ROBIN

Affirmation

'I allow the overlighting consciousness of the robin to open my heart. I acknowledge that I am love. Nothing that is not love will express itself through me. I release all hostility. I want to be a channel for the expression of Divine Love.'

Robin

Robin energy is the energy of pure love. Seeing a robin always brings a lift to the heart. Pure love is without judgement and that is the gift of the robin.

Robins play a very important role in grounding a particular consciousness on earth. Because they express pure love, their presence is like a blessing.

You tap into robin energy whenever you experience a love that is without personal gratification. This is the love that goes beyond romantic love. It is the pure love of the Divine pouring through an open vessel. We are bathed in that love every moment of our lives but very few people can open themselves enough to allow it to express itself through them. Robin consciousness pours that pure love energy through itself and thereby uplifts everything around it.

If you are a robin person, then you are profoundly important on this planet as a pure vessel for Divinity to express itself through. You may do this in very quiet ways; like the robin you are not loud and brash about the gifts you offer, but those around you recognise you by the lift of their hearts in your presence.

Drawing this card in answer to a question or as a daily reading reminds you that personal salvation comes through the development of the ability to love without judgement. Are you closing your heart to someone at the moment because you feel your expectations or needs are not being met? Take a step on your own personal journey and let go the resentment that is closing you off from expressing love. The unfoldment of your heart is a slow process of releasing time and again all the negative emotions that cut you off from allowing love to flow through you.

The blessing of the robin is that it can help you at each stage of the unfoldment, to release the negativity and experience a greater and greater ability to love. Call on the consciousness of the robin in these situations, and watch the blockages melt like snow in the sunshine. Robin consciousness is perfectly aligned with Divine Love and is designed to help you get in touch with your own Divine nature, so let robin enter your heart today.

4 HAWK **4**

Affirmation

'I call upon the overlighting consciousness of hawk to be with me now. I ask for help to break through my situation. I move forward now to total resolution of this issue, with boldness and confidence.'

Hawk

Hawk energy is the energy of the chase. It brings focus and adrenaline into any situation. It heightens awareness of the details involved and allows one to hone in on the essentials. It is a wonderful energy to draw on whenever something is pressing to be attended to. On a higher level, hawk energy can give the spiritual seeker the lift that is needed to break through a difficult situation and reach a desired goal. It focuses the energy and presses through to the conclusion. Don't use hawk energy casually. If you invoke the consciousness of hawk into a situation, then expect a powerful ally.

If hawk is your own personal symbol, then you are a person who loves to command. You have strong leadership qualities and exert control over others easily. Your strength is your ability to bring events to a desired conclusion, through the strength of your will and your focused effort. You are a great asset in any charged situation because you take swift decisions and move the situation forward to resolution. You are a very strong and determined person. Hawk people are less concerned than most people about what others think of them. They know what has to be done, and they produce the results regardless of popular opinion.

You have drawn hawk as your card today because you are needing help to energise your situation. You need to lift the energy purposefully out of the tired state that it is in. Do this by asking the overlighting consciousness of hawk to be there for you. Sometimes the response to this request can be felt very dramatically, other times there is a slow stirring and movement in the situation, but you can be sure that help will come.

You may be wondering if a certain bird of prey that seems to have made a significant appearance in your life, can be identified as a hawk. Hawk energy is the consciousness expressed through all the smaller birds of prey, whatever they are called. Eagle energy has a presence of its own. You go beyond your previous barriers with the help of hawk consciousness. Life is a constant movement upwards towards higher and higher levels of consciousness. Hawk can give you the lift that pulls you up to the next level of expression of yourself.

5 **DOVE** **5**

Affirmation

'I wish to align myself with my own highest truth. I ask for the help of the over-lighting consciousness of the dove to shatter my own illusions and bring me to an awareness of the true nature of Reality. I recognise that I am one with all things in this universe. There is no separation. I flow now into total harmony with my own inner being.'

Dove

Dove energy creates wholeness. Whenever something is out of balance dove energy can be used to bring it back into harmony with itself. Pigeon energy is similar to dove energy but is more concerned with freeing up toxic energy, whereas dove energy harmonises and aligns the energy in its environment.

Doves go where people are congregated because they know where they are needed. The dove symbol has always been associated with peace and hope for the future. Dove energy materialises good around it – that is why peace organisations very appropriately make use of dove peace signs. Look at the truth behind the statement 'as gentle as a dove.' Dove energy is soft and beautiful. It has the effect of helping unite opposites. The sound of doves cooing has a natural harmonising effect on the subtle bodies of people, and people will naturally gravitate towards a place where dove sound predominates, to unwind.

You have been drawn to this card today because something in your life is out of alignment. You know in your heart what this is. Dove energy is gentle, but don't mistake gentleness for lack of power. There is a sweetness to the power of the dove, but it is an effective power nonetheless. If you call on the overlighting consciousness of the dove to help you to bring your life back to harmony, you can expect miracles. The dove works with the Cosmic Christ to bring polarities back to oneness.

If you feel that the dove is your own personal bird symbol, then you have already been lifting the consciousness of your environment in some way. You may be a healer, or simply a loving person, but you are making a profound impact on your environment just by being there. The energy of your presence automatically harmonises the atmosphere of whatever place you find yourself in, even if you are not conscious of it. Some of you may be working very consciously with your energy, to bring balance into people's lives, or to mediate between warring opposites. You have a natural ability to bring about wholeness within whatever situation you place yourself and life is truly grateful for your services. Dove people generate the consciousness of the Cosmic Christ, lifting people up out of their perception of being separate from one another, to the reality of the interconnectedness and oneness of all things.

6 SPARROW **6**

Affirmation

'I ask the overlighting consciousness of the sparrow to fill my heart with its ability to reach out and connect to people in a spirit of companionship. I let go of my past now and accept happily the promise of rich and rewarding associations with my friends and family.'

Sparrow

You have drawn the card of the sparrow today because you are in need of companionship. The sparrow is the bird which expresses the energy of friendship. There are many different species which can be called sparrow in this context. The sparrow energy is friendly and comforting. Sparrows are not dramatically beautiful or alluring but their presence provides a sweet resonance, which can lift one out of feeling low. Having sparrows around your garden brings a quality of merriment and sparkle into your life.

Sparrow people, who feel that the sparrow is the bird that is their special symbol, are wonderful friends. The gift that they offer is true companionship, given without the need to prove anything or without expecting anything in return. All they ask is that they are precious to someone. Friendship is the elixir of life to them and vital to their wellbeing. Sparrow people cannot exist happily in a place where they are surrounded by people who are cool and aloof. They need the warm, friendly interchange that enables them to feel connected to life.

If you have drawn this card in answer to a question, then be alert to the subject of friendship in your life. Are you perhaps denying a sparrow person in your environment the personal contact that he or she desperately needs? Maybe you yourself are feeling down and need to make the effort to connect with someone to lift you out of your despondency. Don't deny the importance of just being near people. Places where lots of people congregate can be wonderfully therapeutic for someone who is in private anguish. Have you lost your party spirit lately? Let the overlighting consciousness of the gregarious sparrow bring the zest back into your life. You can invite the consciousness of the sparrow to pour its warm, busy, ebullient energy into your energy bodies. Sparrows love to be asked to help and you can be sure of their ready response to your appeal.

Friendship is precious and needs to be nurtured. Give a thought to your place in the world. Are you connected to people properly? Do you put enough energy into keeping your friendships and warm connections alive? This question may be the answer to why you are feeling friendless or alone at the moment. You must fill your life with warm, loving, people-connections; then you will know the merriment of the sparrow.

7   PARROT   **7**

Affirmation

'I ask the overlighting consciousness of the parrot to help me to pull away from my own way of looking at my situation and give me a higher perspective. Help me to understand what is really going on. I truly am in control of my life. I choose to feel whatever I am feeling at this moment, and I can choose to actively change that feeling into a higher expression of who I am.'

Parrot

The parrot's energy is more elevated than its squawking behaviour might suggest. Parrots are the masters of the bird kingdom. They carry a very high level of awareness, which perceives the humour inherent in life, and the irony behind the façade of living. Having a parrot in your home can face you with yourself in some rather uncomfortable ways!

If you perceive yourself as resonating to the parrot, then you are not someone who goes along with majority opinion. You have your own ideas on life, and tend to be a wry observer of popular culture. You do not care too much about being perceived as an outsider, because it suits you to be able to watch life rather than participate in it. This gives you the ability to see things as they really are, and have a good chuckle to yourself in the process!

You have drawn this card today because life is asking you to delve a little deeper into your current situation. Look at the true meaning behind what is happening and don't assume that what you are seeing in front of you is all that you need to be perceiving. So often the truth behind a situation needs to be seen from a higher vantagepoint. Changing your perspective can show you a different solution or a different attitude, and often allows you to see the humour in the situation as well. We all take ourselves far too seriously. Let the overlighting consciousness of the parrot lift you to a place where you see things clearly and as they really are.

Parrots are the first birds to spring to mind when thinking of the most suitable bird pet as a companion for someone. This is because they listen and respond. Budgies carry some of the same energies as parrots, as do parakeets, but the energy is less masterful. Lovebirds express something unique and have a card of their own. The memory of a parrot is totally unique in the bird kingdom, and this is what enables them to be so perceptive.

You learn from your mistakes, and in the same way the parrot can learn to build on its past experiences, because of its ability to remember. Similarly, parrot people are able to use their sense of patterns from the past, and tend not to repeat old lessons. This enables them to lead fruitful lives as masters rather than victims of their circumstances.

THRUSH

(8)   (8)

Affirmation

'I accept that my life is out of harmony at the moment. I invite the overlighting consciousness of the thrush to connect with me and help me to find how to bring the harmony back into my life. Show me how to lift myself up to a higher resonance, where I can experience myself as a happy person. I trust that there is a solution, and that I will find it.'

Thrush

Thrush energy is happy energy. Thrushes bring a quality of light-hearted effervescence into their habitat. Don't expect restful energy around a thrush – it is a very busy creature, hopping about in search of interesting worms and other tasty tidbits. All thrushes are excellent parents, taking enormous care over bringing up their offspring.

Thrush song is very lovely. The charm of the thrush's song captivates all who are lucky enough to hear it. It is so melodious that it lifts the tone of the entire region where it can be heard. Heavy hearts lift and pause for a moment in wonder at such beauty. Healing through sound is the mission of the overlighting consciousness of the thrush, and its bursts of song are a gift to the planet and its inhabitants.

People who identify with the thrush as their own symbol are likewise involved in some way with the healing power of beautiful sound. Although the lark and the nightingale are also associated with exquisite song, it is the thrush which specifically uses its voice for healing. The tones and melodies it chooses have been chosen by the overlighting consciousness to be the appropriate ones for that situation. It offers its voice as a balm for the discordant and fractured energies in its environment. Thrush people are also wonderful to have around as their happy, light-hearted presence always brings a lift to the prevailing energy and helps to harmonise the discordant elements in a group situation.

You have drawn this card today, perhaps in answer to a question, or as a daily reading because at some level you are in need of a new sound. You need to identify the discordant tones in your life. The card has come up for you today because the timing is right to find the antidote. It may mean literally finding the right music to lift you out of your current heaviness, or it may rather be speaking metaphorically. Ask the overlighting consciousness of the thrush to help you to identify the discordance, and find the perfect antidote. That is its mission in life, and it will study the situation and help you to see the solution. Tapping into its energy will also help you to feel lighter and more joyous, which in itself is part of the solution. Happy people draw luck and laughter towards them, which naturally helps any situation to feel much better.

9 **BLACKBIRD** **9**

Affirmation

'Today I re-establish my own personal boundaries. I call upon the overlighting consciousness of the blackbird to help me to achieve this. I reaffirm that only those people who hold my best interests in their hearts can enter my private space. I am absolutely safe.'

Blackbird

9

For the purposes of these cards we will put the blackbird and the starling together, because energetically they perform the same function.

Blackbirds are powerful allies for humans on an energy level, even though it so often seems that they are at odds with us. Energetically they perform the same function as the weeds of the plant kingdom – they create a protective layer which helps the more delicate species have time to get strong enough to flourish. They are bossy and fearless, and will chase away predators with remarkable courage. This benefits all the birds in the area that they are protecting. We need the gentle energy of the dove, the cleansing impact of the pigeon, the love energy of the robin, the friendship of the sparrow, and the beautiful harmonies of the thrush, for our own sense of well-being and connection to nature, and this is where the blackbird or starling is our ally.

If you have drawn this card today in response to a question, or as a daily reading, then this is a day when you need to be bold and fearless, and prepared to defend your turf. Don't allow predatory people to overstep the boundaries that are appropriate for you. Make your response quite unmistakable so that the line does not get crossed again. You have an opportunity today to set up the energy structures that will allow you to feel safe. Use the starling or blackbird energy to establish your boundaries clearly, so that you cannot be imposed upon again.

A person who can relate to the blackbird or starling as his or her own special bird, is a very helpful person to have around. He or she may seem abrasive on the surface and may have difficulty communicating other than belligerently, but when the chips are down, a person of this nature is exactly whom you want as your friend or ally. In fact, under that tough exterior is a lovely, warm, humanitarian soul, who gives in so many ways, but who is often misunderstood and under-appreciated.

If there is such a person in your environment, do not be repelled by what you see on the surface. There is so much to be gained from breaking through that hard shell. If you can wait around long enough to start noticing the deep concern for others that is really there, you might find yourself with a friend who is there for you long after everyone else has mysteriously evaporated.

10 **CROW** **10**

Affirmation

'I acknowledge the message that I have received today, and thank the over-lighting consciousness of the crow for bringing it to my attention.'

or

'I call on the overlighting consciousness of crow to be here right now. I am in urgent need of help and protection. I know that you will protect me. I am safe.'

Crow

Crows are bearers of messages from the other worlds. If a crow makes its presence felt to you, take the time to stop and welcome it. Ask it what you should be hearing and see if you can sense the message that it bears. Crows have a reputation for being messengers of doom, but they do not deserve this – they are simply the carriers of guidance from friends in other dimensions.

Crows are also associated with protection. Calling on the overlighting consciousness of the crow when one is feeling threatened will bring the protection that is needed. Despite the harshness of its voice, the real nature of the crow is to help. There is a warmth and humour to the crow's presence, which is similar to the parrot's ironic perception of the strange antics of human beings. Both of them have a high level of consciousness in the bird kingdom.

If you are someone who identifies strongly with the crow as your own symbol, then you are a strong personality, with esoteric interests. You may well be functioning already as a medium, transmitting messages from the astral plane to people in need of guidance or comfort. Even if you are not actively doing this, you would have the undeveloped potential for this kind of work. Your assistance is very much appreciated by those on other dimensions of existence, who struggle to get their thoughts across to those living in the much denser medium of the physical plane.

The message for you today, if you have drawn this card in answer to a question, or as a daily reading, is that you are connected to someone on a different dimension from the physical, who is needing to be in touch with you. It may be an offering of support and protection, or there may be a specific message for you. Find a quiet space for yourself and see if you can hear what is being offered. It doesn't have to come in words – there may be a comforting image, or simply a warm feeling of support. Don't get too intense about getting a whole message; just relax and trust that whatever you need to receive will be imparted in some way or other.

Crows and magpies carry a very similar energy, and are interchangeable with one another for the purposes of these cards.

11   PEACOCK   **11**

Affirmation

'I invite the overlighting consciousness of the peacock and peahen to bring me the vision that I need now to move forward. I ask God to bless my life. I will remember that I am not alone.'

Peacock

11

The peacock and his mate the peahen carry the powerful vibration of God's all-seeing wisdom. The beautiful plumage and tail of the peacock are glorious reminders of the exquisiteness that is the expression of God in nature. Our world is a wonderful playground for God to be expressed in countless different forms and colours – each one unique but also absolutely a part of the whole.

Peacock people are the seers and visionaries of our world. They are the ones we turn to when we need spiritual guidance and counselling. Their wisdom and perceptiveness are the beacons that light our way on the long journey back to our re-awakening to our God-self. If you have a peacock person in your life, treasure him or her. They are very rare birds indeed.

If you have drawn the peacock card today, then you are blessed. It is a day when you may feel the power of God's blessing directly, as an actual physical experience, or through unexpected little miracles that bring you joy. Hold the thought in your heart today that you are deeply loved, by an all-seeing Presence who knows exactly who you are, and where you belong. No-one is ever truly alone, because that all-seeing eye is with you in every moment.

Peacocks and peahens represent the aspect of God that brings understanding into the world. This is not meant as book-learning, but the deep heart-wisdom that comes through battling with the paradoxes of life.

Joy comes through finding the way beyond the paradox of opposites to the still centre where all is one. The single eye of the peacock's tail is the I within which everything in the universe resides. The overlighting consciousness of the peacock and peahen can be called upon to help you to take the next step of your journey toward your Self.

12 SWAN **12**

Affirmation

'I ask the overlighting consciousness of the swan to help me with this relationship. Teach me how to create true balance within myself, so that my outer partnership reflects this inner equilibrium. I know that I am exactly where I am meant to be at this moment, and I honour the gifts that this partnership brings.'

Swan

Swans are delicate creatures. Their grace and beauty are legendary, and their serene presence is a wonderful gift to any lake or river. The true gift of the swan is its ability to know its partner for life. Once mated, the male or female swan will not mate again with any other swan, even if its mate dies. It is as if its mate has imprinted itself upon its soul, and no other image will do in its place.

Your card today is speaking to you of partnership. It is the most profound blessing to find one's true partner in life, but not everyone is destined to do so. Sometimes the lesson is to develop your own inner masculine or feminine side, so that you have the experience of the sacred marriage within your own being, and do not look to an outside partner to complete you. Each person has to achieve this wholeness within, whether or not he or she is involved in an outer partnership as well. It is an essential precondition for the final stages of Self-realisation. Very often, the inner marriage of the male and female elements within your own psyche will set the stage for the outer meeting with your true partner; you are ready for true commitment at a soul level. Look at the reality of your relationship with your current partner. Try to feel what it is that this partnership is offering you. Every partnership brings its own gifts, and it is a rare partnership that feels completely perfect. Before you put this card away, verbalise to yourself at least one powerful reason why you are together.

No-one really knows for sure what life has in store for the future. Honour your partner and make full use of your time together. Don't leave loving words unsaid or put off fulfilling your shared dreams. Romance may seem a little tired between you, but the true glue of a loving partnership is friendship. This may not be your true soul marriage, or maybe it is, but either way, if you can be true friends to one another, you have found the key to successful partnership.

People who identify with the swan as their own particular symbol are deeply committed to the partnership they find themselves in. Honouring this partnership is one of the primary joys of their life. This is usually a union of two people who have gone a long way toward the balancing of their own inner masculine and feminine polarities, so that the outer marriage is serene and full of grace. Ask the overlighting consciousness of the swan to help you in your quest for this state of grace.

13 EAGLE **13**

Affirmation

'I ask for the presence of the overlighting consciousness of the eagle in my life. With this presence overlighting me, I will reclaim my power. It is done.'

Eagle

13

Eagles fly to a height beyond that which most birds reach. They see huge vistas far below them and are able to track tiny creatures with their incredible eyesight. They are the kings and queens of the bird kingdom and they carry the vibrational energy of the power aspect of God. (Peacocks and peahens carry the wisdom aspect of God, and the robin carries the love aspect.)

Huge power is at the disposal of kings and queens, and so it is with people who resonate to the eagle as their symbol. These are the people who are natural-born leaders. If they are already mature souls, they will rule others with wisdom and compassion, but there are also eagle types who display the more predatory aspects of the eagle's nature, and abuse their power. If you are an eagle person, know that your power has been bestowed upon you by God alone. If you allow God to work through you, your might has the power of Divinity behind it, but if you do not align yourself with God's presence in your life, you can crash rather spectacularly in a spiritual sense – because power is an enormous magnifier of both the good and the bad elements in your personality.

You have drawn this eagle card today, in answer to a question or as a daily reading, because this is a day for taking back your power. With the help of the overlighting consciousness of the eagle, you can seize control of your life again. Eagles fly high and scan the area below them. They have a much better sense of the whole picture than we do on the ground. Perceive your area of powerlessness and forcefully reclaim what is lost.

History is full of the stories of the rise and fall of great empires. These are the conquests of the eagle people, who know that their path to wisdom is to learn to handle the trappings and temptations of great power with humility. This can play itself out in the world of temporal power, but also applies just as much to spiritual power. The magi of the spiritual world are contending with huge temptations to misuse the power at their disposal as well. Sexual energy is a frequently lethal pitfall for both temporal and spiritual power mongers. It is a truly great soul who manages to avoid these potential traps and reaches the dizzy heights of spiritual conquest.

14 OWL **14**

Affirmation

'Today is a day for deep change at a soul level. I acknowledge the overlighting consciousness of the owl and seek its help in the release of my old patterns. Help me to connect with the spiritual forces that will best guide me to a place within myself where I am in touch with joy.'

Owl

14

Night creatures like the owl represent the collective unconscious of mankind. This is the place where our true knowing resides. There is mystery here, and magic. We are unconscious of the life of these shy birds, because we are asleep, but while we dream they swoop and call and hunt and watch.

Have you had an owl flit through your life today? To see an owl is always portentous. It gives notice that big events are at hand. Traditionally, owls bring forewarning of a death, but it is more likely the death of a way of living – some kind of important transition is on its way. Don't see this as something to dread; transitions can take you to wonderful new opportunities.

If you have chosen this owl card in answer to a question, or as a daily reading, then life is saying that there are subterranean movements in your life that are bringing about some kind of change. Be mindful of this, and know that whatever is coming has its own timing. You may be pushing for major changes and frustrated that nothing seems to be happening. The owl card is telling you to relax and allow greater forces than your own will to move mountains for you. Hasty action at this time might thwart the slow coming together of supportive structures that need to be in place first. Do not suppose that because nothing is happening, nothing is happening! Happy events are just as often presaged by an owl's appearance as transitions are. Remember that the owl represents the collective unconscious forces at work in people's psyches. This means that there is a connection between one person and another at an unconscious level. We are all sharing the same nightmares and fears and anxieties, but we also share powerful archetypal images which bind us together in a common language that is not spoken but felt deeply as the common language of humanity. Soul work involves delving deeply into one's own unconscious to root out the deeply imbedded negative patterns that have been inherited, or imbedded through one's response to painful events. Once these negative patterns have been erased, the soul can find positive ones to put consciously in their place. It is a conscious effort of will needed to replace a dark influence with a lighter one. As more and more of the dark in the psyche is infused with light, it is possible for spiritual forces to start working powerfully within the individual. This connects him or her with guiding forces in the universe which can steer his or her course through life with less pain.

15 STORK **15**

Affirmation
'I invite the overlighting consciousness of the stork to work with me in bringing my project to completion. I see it finished, and I know it can be done.'

Stork

15

Traditionally, the stork delivers the baby. Hidden behind this beguiling myth is the truth of what the stork consciousness is working with on an energy level. Stork energy provides the focused power that helps to bring a creative event into physical manifestation. It takes energy and will power to take an idea from the level of thought and bring it through so that it has life in the world. Stork energy can help you to land your baby in the world, exactly where it is meant to be.

What is it that you are trying to bring into manifestation at the moment? This card is suggesting that there is some brainchild that you are trying to make real in the physical world. You would have a great ally in the stork. Invite the overlighting consciousness of the stork into your particular situation, and allow it time to work through the obstacles that are hindering the deliverance of this particular project. You can significantly speed up the gestation period this way!

If you identify strongly with the stork as your own symbol, then you are notable for bringing your ideas to fruition. You have a gift for taking an idea right through from the initial concept to its appearance as a reality in the world. This takes will power, clarity of focus, and determination. Acknowledge your remarkable ability to deliver – not everyone is blessed with this asset.

Stork energy can be utilised at the deepest level of the psyche, to help to work through the obstacles that are holding the self back from merging with the Self. Its focused, purposeful energy can be extremely powerful here. If you feel drawn to the stork or it appears magically in your life in some way, then do invite it into your life, to work with you in bringing to birth your own perfect Self.

16 **LARK** **16**

Affirmation

'I know now that there is no point in holding onto my pain any longer. I ask God to be the judge of this situation, and I let go of my own need to mete out justice. I let go of my hurt so that I can let in the joy of life. I ask the overlighting consciousness of the lark to lift me up to Heaven and I invite in all the bliss and joy that life can offer, to set me free from pain.'

Lark

16

Larks are clarion calls from the world of nature to our world. They bring the message of redemption through abandoning oneself to joy. The lark ascends on its exquisite song of joy and becomes one with its maker in its ecstasy. There is no pain in its path to Heaven, only the delight of participating in a joyous celebration of life.

Lark serves us by reminding us of the power of sheer exultation. Bliss comes from abandoning ourselves completely to waves of joy. Holding onto pain creates a barrier against the healing power of joy and bliss, and we keep ourselves stuck in melancholia and heartache through our stubborn refusal to give in, and give up the past. We love to hang onto every last little bit of hurt and anger and prolong our suffering interminably this way. Lark is reminding you just to let go. Let go of all the misery and bitterness. Release the pent-up fury and resentment. Give in to the song of life that so badly wants to lift you up to the heavens, if only you would allow it to flow through you and heal your wounds.

If you have chosen the lark card today, then please listen to its song of joy. Allow the transcendent music of this little bird to transport you to an experience of blissful union with the Divine. You are holding onto something, and it is time to let it go. Let God deal with the wrongdoers, and do not hurt yourself by holding onto grievances.

If you resonate to the lark as your own symbol, then you know the power of exultation. You know how to let joy run through your body cells and flush out all the poisons. You probably sing like a diva, and can raise the rooftops with your magnificent singing ability. Lark people use sound to take themselves to the goal of ultimate union with the Divine, and give a lot of people pleasure in the process. They do not use their sound as an antidote to negativity as the thrush does, but as their own path to joy. However, their sheer glorification of sound can show others how to let go into undiluted joyousness.

17   NIGHTINGALE   **17**

Affirmation

'I let go of the form of that which hurts me, and allow in the love of God instead. I ask the overlighting consciousness of the nightingale to reveal that which is true. I accept God as my true love.'

Nightingale

Have you ever heard a nightingale sing? It is the most thrilling, heart-stopping sound. Nightingales sing to us of the reality behind the illusion of life. It stops our heart for a moment, because we are in the illusion while our hearts beat, and we have forgotten. We have forgotten that life is a song that God is singing in every moment. God is expressing the sheer joy of creating universe upon universe of wonders and miracles. And every particle of that universe is loved. The nightingale reminds us that while we think we suffer and weep, our universe is singing all the time. If we could but tune into that song, our suffering would just evaporate – because suffering is the illusion that we are separated from God. We think we have been thrown out of the garden in shame and disgrace, and that we have to clothe ourselves and hide our faces from God. God is there in every particle of matter, in every moment. It is our illusion that we are separated from Divine Love. If we can let go of our shame and let that Divine Love into our lives again, we will start to hear the song of the nightingale in our own hearts.

People who resonate to the nightingale as their own special bird, are way beyond most people in their power to activate Divine Love. The robin pours Divine Love through itself into the world, just by opening itself and becoming an empty vessel for Love to pour through. The nightingale actively releases love in the cells of the creatures who hear its song. The song resonates so closely with the continuous Song of God, that all who hear it are subtly changed. Nightingale people have this rarefied ability to change those around them through the power of their love.

If you have chosen the nightingale card today, then you may be engaged in a life-changing inner drama. Nightingale energy is powerfully transformatory, and can bring you to your resolution with swift assistance. Allow it to enter your dilemma, and see how the power of Divine Love shatters the illusions and reveals what is Real.

You have a choice today: hold onto your attachment to God clothed in a particular form, or let go of that form and discover that instead of losing something, you have gained the only true lover – God, who is in all things.

IBIS

Affirmation

'It is time for me to know myself. I invite the overlighting consciousness of the ibis to merge with my own consciousness and show me God. I release all resistance to my full Self being revealed to me. I am ready.'

Ibis

18

Ibis reveals the heart of the matter. The sacred ibis, the hadeda ibis and the other members of the ibis family are carrying a vibration that cries out to the world that there is a joke here that we are missing. The raucous cries of the hadeda ibis mock us with our self-appointed sense of being the ones who make the decisions. You are not who you think you are. You are much, much, more incredible than you have any inkling of. The ibis laughs at the ridiculousness of the vastness of ourselves living as if we were moles – blind and tunneling in the dark, when all around us there is light.

Drawing the ibis card is very, very significant. It is your Self calling you back home. It is the signal that who you think you are is about to discover who you really are. Ibis is about to reveal its punchline – the joke is on us.

You cannot hold back the tide of the revealing of the Self to the self. The self quivers because it thinks it will lose itself, but it can only hold back the tide for so long. The mighty force of the Self knows no barriers. At the appointed moment it will crash through the ego's terrified resistance and the full glory of who you are will be revealed. And then you will laugh with the ibis.

If you resonate to the ibis as your own special symbol, then you are a giant of the world of spiritual leadership. You are truly with God. You know who you are, and understand the joke that the ibis proclaims.

Ibis people can see beyond the apparent manifestation of reality. They know the real truth that lies at the heart of it all. No one can con them into believing that they are less than what they are. They live that truth. So will we all one day.

If the ibis is clamoring for your attention, know that your Self awaits. Allow ibis to remind you that the real you is radiant beyond description, and vast. So vast that it is actually no different from God, because God is all that there is. When you know that, then you know your Self.

19 **FINCH** **19**

Affirmation

'I ask for the help of the overlighting consciousness of the finch to perceive my true purpose in this community. In what way can I best serve Self here?"

Finch

The little finch has no sense of itself as separate from the whole. Its entire experience is played out as part of a flock; the consciousness of the flock is one consciousness, and the little birds are all expressions of that one consciousness. At no moment does a finch feel itself to be outside that great consciousness that lives through it. In the same way, each of us is actually part of that huge consciousness that is God. As human beings, unlike the finch, we split ourselves off from the awareness of that continuity of consciousness, and believe ourselves to be separate and alone.

Like the finch, we function as one precious part of a much greater whole, and we are responding and communicating with it all the time, to greater and lesser degrees of awareness. People who resonate to the finch as their favourite bird symbol are living their lives as part of a community. Their need is to offer their skills to the good of the whole, and by doing this they are deeply fulfilled. They are usually very harmonious people, who can blend in with others without imposing their own way of doing things too much. Communities demand particular kinds of rigorous inner work, and for many people can be a powerful path to Self-realisation. There are many temptations and many pitfalls along the way, and one can be faced with oneself in most uncomfortable ways.

If you have drawn the finch card today, then look at what is happening in relation to the particular community situation in your own life. You may not actually be living in a community, but most people belong to some kind of community situation, whether it be church, neighbourhood, school, or simply a group of friends. What is it that needs to shift in your awareness to bring greater harmony to your situation? Is the shadow side of your personality causing harm to others or trying to impose its own will to the detriment of the whole?

Or, is someone else's shadow side impacting in a negative way on you? It may be that the growth is to recognise that it is time to move on. Ask the overlighting consciousness of the finch to help you to know whether it is in your best interests to stay, and work through the issues confronting you here, or whether it is time to free yourself from this particular community, and move into a new cycle in your life. Your soul knows the answer.

CANARY

(20)   (20)

Affirmation

'I ask the overlighting consciousness of the canary to be with me now. I allow its optimistic energy to put me back on the path to joy. I ask God to bless my situation and help me to move forward. I know there is a solution and that I will be shown the way.'

Canary

20

Canary energy is sun energy. It is the bright life-affirming energy that warms all things. Canaries are loved by people as pets, because their lovely yellow colour and pretty song are like tiny little sources of sunshine for us in our homes. Canary-lovers need to have their hearts lifted by these creatures; they instinctively choose the energy that will help them rise above whatever dreariness is dragging them down.

People who resonate to the canary as their own symbol are happy-go-lucky troubadours. Their nature is warm and cheerful, and always brings a lift to the people around them. They usually love singing, and can easily create music from whatever instrument they choose. People naturally gravitate towards them to share in their warmth and vitality. Sunshine energy is optimistic energy and this is a great boon to any situation. Canary people are sensitive souls, who can use their life-affirming energy to help people in pain. All canaries have the facility to lift people out of melancholia and back into harmony with themselves. Many canary people therefore work in places where their gift is needed, like hospitals or really bleak, poverty-stricken environments.

The important point about canary people is that the life-affirming energy they carry is not consciously projected. It is just part of them, and beams out of them regardless of who they are with. It is especially effective therefore in situations where people need to feel unconditionally accepted – like prisons, or mental institutions, or any down-and-out environment. These are the gifted souls who really make a difference.

If you have chosen the canary card today, then be optimistic. Assume the best possible outcome for your particular situation. Allow the lovely canary yellow to warm you and give you hope. Hope automatically brings balance back into your situation and allows you to see your position realistically and without the blinkers of gloom and despondency.

Revitalise yourself now by asking the overlighting consciousness of the sweet canary to pour its resonance into your energy fields. Fill yourself with the colour yellow, and go and find some light and sunshine to balance your soul.

21 FLAMINGO **21**

Affirmation

'This situation is worthy of my energy and attention. I invite the overlighting consciousness of the flamingo to guide me to my best function within this group of people, and I ask for help in letting go of my personal ambitions so that I can offer my services to the greater good of the whole.'

Flamingo

Flamingos are nearly always found in colonies. It is rare to see them by themselves. They make such a spectacular sight as a group – the individual is so much less than the sum of its parts. Flamingo energy speaks to us of nationhood. It is the combined effect of so many different individual parts that makes the beauty of the whole. It is love energy that is the coalescing force between any group of people, and the soft flamingo pink resonates powerfully to love.

If you have drawn the flamingo card today, in answer to a question, or as a daily reading, then ask yourself where in your life you could be adding your energy to a situation to improve its power. Many of us tend to hold back from fully engaging in situations, because we cannot see that our energy would make any difference. The flamingo card is saying that there is a situation where adding your energy will make a big difference. It is not that you yourself are likely to receive any credit for the difference you make, but you will know in your own heart that your energy was engaged purposefully. Your reward will be to see that the whole situation moves forward in some way and to know that you were a part of that.

People who resonate to the flamingo as their own special bird, feel the need to offer their energies to a greater cause than just their own individual advancement. These are the politicians, and the fighters for justice everywhere, who often go unnoticed, but who have laid down their own individual lives in service to a greater objective. Pink is the colour of love, and for this offering of oneself to be truly successful, it must be done with openhearted humility. If the personal ego is allowed to overshadow the situation, then much can be lost, and the whole situation may be thrown off balance because your individual ambition is wanting to be fed.

Ask the overlighting consciousness of the flamingo to keep you humble. Remember that you are only one little part in a very big whole. You are needed, but only if you add your energy to the situation, and not if you are there to be noticed.

22 PELICAN **22**

Affirmation

'I invite the overlighting consciousness of the pelican to hold my hand today as I walk through this pain. I know that I have to let go of .... Help me to release .... and feel the joy of freedom from something that is trapping me on the physical plane of existence.'

Pelican

Pelicans are the birds who resonate closest to the energy of material acquisition. It is not fundamentally wrong to acquire material possessions. The only thing one truly possesses is one's Self – that is all there is. The sage knows this and is able to live in the world of matter without attachment; whether rich or poor, he or she is identified only with his or her true nature – possessions come and go, to be enjoyed, but not hung on to.

People who resonate closely to the pelican as their bird symbol have reached this positive state of being with regard to material possessions. They may hoard many beloved objects, just as the pelican stores up food in its beak – but they have let go of their attachment to the form of these things. They can enjoy the ownership of something with no horror at the thought of maybe having to lose it. This is a blessed state of being; it allows the person to play with the toys of the physical world without being ensnared by them. The pull of the form of things is so great, however, that it is only very mature souls who truly are able to be in this state of grace with regard to their possessions. Most of us fall very far short of this ideal.

You have drawn the pelican card today, in answer to a question, or as a daily reading, to alert you to an inappropriate attachment in your life at the moment. Who or what are you holding on to? You can use the compassionate energy of the pelican to help you to realise the inappropriateness of this attachment, and to let go. If you can make an inner shift of awareness that lets you see that all is God, and that all you are letting go of is the form of something, rather than its essence, then you will manage to release this thing or person much more easily.

Pelicans really understand the principle of hoarding and letting go, and you will be gently assisted through the process if you ask for their help. Remember that all there is is Self, and therefore nothing can ever be truly lost.

23   KINGFISHER   **23**

Affirmation

'I welcome the overlighting consciousness of the kingfisher into my heart. I am ready to remember.'

Kingfisher

23

Kingfishers live near lakes and rivers. They live in the trees and fly in the air, but are dependent on the water for their food. The energy of the kingfisher is deeply transformatory. They are the bird equivalents of the holy people of our world. Their deeply spiritual essence penetrates our materiality and reminds us of our non-physical purpose. Holy men and women offer their grace to the world to help to lift people up to a greater level of spiritual understanding. The overlighting consciousness of the kingfisher is a vast being, who works within nature to offer a particular tone, which allows those who can tune into it an opportunity to realise their true nature once again.

Those who resonate to the kingfisher as their own special symbol, are quietly transmuting dull lead into glowing gold in everything they impact on around them. Their presence is a blessing and their effect is like a ripple in an infinite ocean, that just expands outwards into eternity.

If you have drawn the kingfisher card today, then you are connecting with your true Self. Something is happening that is drawing the veils aside and is allowing you to remember who you really are. You have been that all the time, but the illusion of the physical world has persuaded you otherwise. Now you know.

24   **SEAGULL**   **24**

Affirmation

'I allow the overlighting consciousness of the seagull to help me to access my unconscious fears and programming. I ask God to be with me in this process. I acknowledge that there can be no healing without the presence of God. I float free.'

Seagull

Imagine being able to fly over the sea, unhindered and unfettered, just looking down at the beautiful vast expanse of water and knowing that you are master of it. You need not fear it, because when you are tired, you just drift down to float for a moment on top of it, or, if you are hungry, you dive down into its depths to grab a fish. There is no sense of being limited to the shore or rooted to the earth. What freedom!

People who resonate to the seagull as their own bird symbol have risen above earthly encumbrances. It is in the realm of the unconscious, symbolised by the sea, that they have to work; to dive into its depths and bring up what is hidden into the light of conscious awareness. These are people who are deeply involved in their own inner work and who probably are not very engaged with the physical world and its glamorous offerings. Their energy is very focused rather on unravelling their inner demons and letting them go, so that the pure Light of spirit can shine through unhindered. This can be a long journey, and can take many years, but once accomplished, there is no longer anything to pull one's attention away from the truth of oneself – and the seagull becomes an albatross – flying unhindered over the stormy seas with no need to land anywhere.

You have drawn the seagull card, because life is showing you where you are going. You are learning to become a seagull, or even an albatross – unfettered by earthly entrapments. You are putting your energy and focus rather on bringing your fears and old negative beliefs out of your unconscious to be healed by the light of your conscious Self. If you are feeling rather weary from the seeming endlessness of this process, take a break. Like the seagull, come to rest for a moment on that infinite ocean that is your own Self, and just remind yourself that you are one with God. In our zeal to unravel all the apparent dark corners of our psyche, we sometimes forget just to turn on the Light. We are not alone, and God is there in every dark corner and in every moment. Don't forget to let the Light of God heal your wounds for you. If you are battling your demons without this Light, then you are still in the illusion that you are separate from God, and there is a real danger of drowning. Ask the overlighting consciousness of the seagull to lift you up again so that you can fly free.

(25) HERON **(25)**

Affirmation

'I wish to work with the overlighting consciousness of the heron from this moment. I commit myself to a process of detoxification. I invite my Spirit to work with me also so that it can be freed from clogging energy.'

Heron

25

Herons are beautiful, elegant creatures. Their energy offers us an opportunity to purify ourselves from unwanted disturbances in our subtle bodies. Think of the cattle egret; its joy and purpose in life is to pick ticks and other insects off the backs of cattle and other large herbivores. Heron energy is a wonderfully helpful energy to tap into when we are needing help to dislodge unwanted behaviour patterns or any kind of stuck, old, energy.

You are likely to recognise yourself as offering heron energy if you work in the world in some kind of cleaning capacity – either literally or metaphorically. You are rinsing off the grime to let in more light, and God loves you for it. Dirt in any form, whether it be in the physical realm, or in the subtler levels of life, drags down the vibrational rate so that the subtle light of God is less able to express itself fully. Cleansing and purification rituals are therefore not empty forms of religion, but extremely effective ways of raising the vibrational level of someone or something so that more of the Spirit can reveal itself.

Choosing the heron card today is a call to purify yourself. Maybe you are being prepared for a major shift in consciousness, or maybe you have allowed an accretion of too much old energy to build up in your system. It may signal a need to look at your diet – perhaps a detoxifying regime is needed.

Whatever it is in your own life that needs lightening up, heron energy will be a wonderful boost to get you going with the process. Invite the overlighting consciousness of the heron to work with you to cleanse the windows of your soul, so that the light of your beautiful Spirit can shine out for all to see.

26 **DUCK** **26**

Affirmation

'I release my hostile attitude to myself from this moment. I align myself with the overlighting consciousness of the duck now, to assist me to be aware of each moment of self-deprecation. I admit that I am precious, and I commit myself to taking care of this precious person through every thought, word and deed that I am responsible for.'

26 *Duck*

We are not very kind to ourselves. All of us, to some degree or other, are constantly pecking at ourselves. There is very little that we give ourselves credit for – that inner dialogue just rips us apart all the time. Have you ever watched a party of ducks swimming together in a pond or river? They squabble and peck at one another ferociously. Duck energy helps us get in touch with our malevolence to ourselves, and then to transmute it to something kinder.

You have drawn the duck card today, in answer to a question, or as a daily reading, because you are being alerted to an aspect of yourself that you are definitely not giving enough credit to. Stop and think for a moment about your life. If it were someone else's life you were looking at, what would you praise him or her for? What would be that person's shining achievements? Would you pat him or her on the back and acknowledge an enormous amount of effort? If you could do it for someone else, please do it right now for yourself.

If you resonate to the duck as your own bird symbol, then you are a person who is extremely hard on yourself. You pull yourself down at every opportunity, and find it very hard to let in praise. You usually put yourself out for others, but allow yourself very little latitude. Your biggest challenge this lifetime is to learn to love yourself. Watch your inner dialogue and see how badly you treat yourself. Every time you pull yourself down, from this moment on, stop that thought and replace it with one that honours you.

The overlighting consciousness of the duck understands deeply about this tendency to hurt ourselves. If you tap into duck energy you will have an ally in the process of becoming alerted to your inner self-destructiveness. Once you notice quite how poisonous your relationship is with yourself, you can start to do something about it. This takes an effort of will, to change thought patterns and automatic responses to more loving ones.

Remember that the true you is nothing less than God. Until you can honour yourself as part of God, God has a pretty hard time getting through to you. As you work at loving yourself, God's love for you can show itself more obviously, and you can start to glow as the radiant being that you really are.

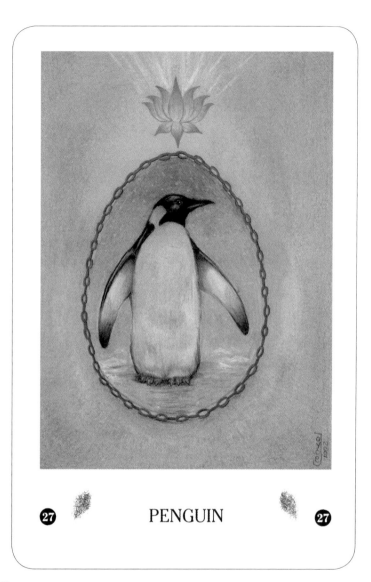

27 PENGUIN **27**

Affirmation
'I am beautiful. There is nothing in my body that is not holy and beloved of God. I ask the overlighting consciousness of the penguin to help me to see myself with the eyes of God. I release my hostility to my body and ask it to receive my love from now on.'

Penguin

The penguin is a very funny bird to watch on land, but swimming underwater to catch a fish presents no problem at all – there is no awkwardness there. Penguin consciousness reflects the energy of the perfect soul trapped in an imperfect body. It can be an enormous help to those who feel trapped in a body that does not work perfectly, or does not fit the accepted perfect form of the day.

People who identify with the penguin as their bird symbol are likely to be uncomfortable with their body in some way. There may be an actual physical handicap or simply a fury that their body is not the perfect model shape. They have usually compensated for this physical discomfort in some way; either by developing their minds powerfully, or going within and finding the freedom of an unfettered spirit. The challenge here is to accept themselves just as they are, imperfect body and all. They have to let go the anger at themselves for being different, and instead learn to love their uniqueness. In this battle they come to learn who they really are.

You have chosen the penguin card today because there is an aspect of your physical body that you are loathing. Please stop for a moment and think what it feels like to be loathed. Your body has a consciousness – it responds to the energies that are directed at it. Every single thing in the universe blossoms and flourishes under the influence of the energy of love, and wilts and dies if exposed to too much hate. Your body is no exception. It can keep going only so long under a bombardment of criticism and rejection. Penguin energy can be your ally in helping you to perceive yourself as beautiful in your own eyes. Once you can really allow yourself to be beautiful just as you are, you will see the holy form of a perfect God or Goddess, radiating through that sacred chalice that is your body. And you will have discovered the Holy Grail

28 PLOVER **28**

Affirmation

'I ask God to be with me as I turn to face my persecutor. I know that I can win this battle. I call upon the overlighting consciousness of the plover to give me courage. I realise my strength and I see my support. I can do this.'

Plover

28

The plover's characteristic feature is the intensity with which it defends its nest and eggs. Running along the ground, it will distract any potential threat by attempting to lead it away from the nest, sometimes even pretending to look vulnerable, with a limp or broken wing, until the predator gets too close, and it flies quickly away. What it offers us on an energy level, therefore, is the ability to foil a powerfully menacing energy that may be threatening us, even though we may look and feel a lot less powerful than the aggressor.

If you have drawn the plover card today, then life is saying that you have it in you to be the one who will be the victor in the situation you find yourself in now. You may seem more fragile, but you have the guile to deftly turn the situation to your advantage. Do not be put off by the apparent might of your opponent – this is a David and Goliath type of situation, and giants can be felled. If you engage the overlighting consciousness of the plover to be your ally here, you will find yourself becoming bold. There is no need to feel as if you have to do this alone – call on the presence of God to assist you, and confidently expect all the support that you need. This card is a sign to you from your helpers and guides that you have the support on an inner level and that you should do battle with this foe. The history of the situation demands that.

People who relate strongly to the plover as their own bird symbol have usually been through the kind of scenario just described. They already know their capacity to come out on top of an apparently impossibly threatening situation. It has given them a strong respect for themselves, and a confidence in being able to draw on support from unseen helpers. They would be able to tell you that when you are honouring Spirit, then Spirit honours you. If you are honouring yourself in this process, and taking back your dignity and self-respect, then you are honouring Spirit. Your ally is the plover, whose energy can be called upon to help you to access your personal power, and triumph.

(29) GOOSE **(29)**

Affirmation

'I am finished. I thank the overlighting consciousness of the goose for its promise of rewards for my long labour, and I hear the applause.'

Goose

29

Goose energy materialises wealth. The story of Jack and the Beanstalk, and the goose that lays the golden eggs, has this message implicit in it. It is wealth that has been earned through battling with inner giants, that is materialised through the goose. Once the giant has been slain, the energy that has up until now been locked up and unusable can pour forth into the world. This brings rich fruits in the form of both material and spiritual wealth.

If you are identifying with the goose as your bird symbol, then you have probably already experienced the rich harvest that goose energy can represent. Heaven has blessed you with visible effect. Slaying your own giant will have cost you a huge amount of tremendously focused inner effort – to overcome your fears and face the whole truth of yourself – but now that the goal has been reached, life pours that energy back into you with no effort on your part at all. Your friends may call you lucky, but you know better; perhaps only you and God know quite what slaying that inner giant really cost you, and you know that what is coming to you now is applause.

Drawing the goose card today signifies the end of a process. It is a triumph. At last you can rest. You are being told, by means of this card, that your giant is overcome, and you can now look forward to a time of bountiful blessings and peace. Well done.

30 CORMORANT **30**

Affirmation

'I invite the overlighting consciousness of the cormorant to be with me today. I hear the need of ... for assistance, and ask God to help him/her to move towards the Light.'   or

'I ask the overlighting consciousness of the cormorant to assist me to shift out of the fear that is keeping me locked into this unhappy situation. I acknowledge that it is time to let go and move on.'

Cormorant

Cormorants have a different energy from seagulls, although both live in similar environments. They offer the gift of helping to release the spirit from the body after death, and guiding the spirit to its destination. They do not do this in their physical form, but in their own spirit bodies. Their energy can be called upon to help someone who is finding it difficult to release from the physical plane after death, or to take someone to a higher level of vibration if they are stuck at an uncomfortable place.

People who feel a particular affinity with cormorant energy may well be doing this kind of rescue work themselves, sometimes without knowing it. Many of us are very active in the spiritual realms at night, and work to assist angelic beings to release trapped souls.

If you have chosen the cormorant card today, then there may be someone who is calling to you to assist them. You will probably know who this is, but if you don't, sit quietly for a while and see if it comes to you. Ask the overlighting consciousness of the cormorant to activate light around this person. Then ask God to send the appropriate helper to guide him or her to the place where he or she will be at peace. You will probably sense a shift of energy as this occurs. Remember to thank all these assisting energies afterwards. You don't have to engage your own energy in this process – you just ask for the most appropriate help.

Cormorant energy is also sometimes the perfect energy for someone in a physical body who is stuck in an uncomfortable place emotionally; it can give the boost that is needed to get life moving again. It is as if the person needs to recognise that the old life he or she has been hanging on to is actually over, and has to be let go of. Cormorant energy can help people to see this, and then to move to a more vibrant expression of themselves.

You may have chosen the cormorant card today because you yourself are the one who needs the help to move out of a stuck place. Fear is always the energy that keeps us from moving forward. Identify your fear – look it full in the face – and then invite the overlighting consciousness of the cormorant to help you to lift yourself out of the prison you are keeping yourself in – high enough to see the endless vistas of sea and sky and beautiful earth, that are yours to play in.

CRANE

31 31

Affirmation

'I invite the overlighting consciousness of the crane to enter into this divisive situation and to bring it to a loving conclusion. I ask it also to cleanse my own heart from the subtle prejudices that still cause me to be separate from others. I embrace…'

Crane

The powerful blessing of the crane is that it carries the energy necessary to transform irrational prejudice into tolerance and understanding. There is no accident in the fact that the exquisite blue crane is the bird symbol for South Africa. The overlighting presence of the crane has been slowly bringing its healing influence to bear on the situation, with astonishing results.

You have drawn this card today because life is wanting to heal something for you. There is some area of your life which is out of balance, because you are needing to inject more sustained loving energy in that direction. Prejudice against someone, or something, means that we are withholding our loving approval from that person, or thing. Any prejudice, however subtle, keeps us in a state of separateness. We cannot experience a mystical union with the Divine if we are withholding love from something. Love asks us to reach out and embrace, not to withhold and reject. You may be very aware of the area of prejudice that this card is bringing to your attention, or you may need to sit and think for a while about where you are having difficulty in blessing a situation.

Once you are clear about the nature of your prejudice, invite the overlighting energy of the crane to enter into the situation, and help you to shift your inner dynamic from that of judgement and polarisation to that of loving compassion. You do not have to agree with something to be tolerant and understanding in your attitude towards it. You simply embrace it in your heart.

If you have regarded the crane as your own bird symbol, then healing the wounds of prejudice is your own special task. You will recognise the way in which this manifests in your life – it may be the work that you do, or you may be in a situation where you are called upon to mediate between clashing factions. People with crane energy are superb at bringing about the dissolution of tension in a polarised situation.

The overlighting energy of the crane is offering itself to the world at this time, because it is so crucial that the barriers of hatred and intolerance between different groups are dissolved. This is a real gift that we can offer our planet; by inviting this consciousness in to help with any divisive situation, big or small, we slowly move from holding on to our differences, to knowing our connectedness, and beyond that to actually feeling the Love that binds us all.

32 HUMMINGBIRD **32**

Affirmation

'I accept joyously that a new dawn is breaking for me. I thank the overlighting consciousness of the hummingbird for opening my vision to see what is there. I know that I have moved on from old constrictions, and that happy outcomes can be real for me.'

Hummingbird

Hummingbirds and sunbirds both carry a very similar energy. They express the joy that is inherent in living and remind us to relish the feast that life offers. Hummingbirds have a different overlighting consciousness from sunbirds, however, and therefore offer a slightly different energy.

Hummingbird energy specifically carries the resonance of freedom from pain and suffering. If you have drawn the hummingbird card today, then you are handling your life in such a way that you are liberating yourself from the heavy chains of the past, and starting to lift into the light of joy. It is a message to you that you are succeeding. Eventually, the light will break through completely, and the bliss will be so overwhelming that pain and suffering can no longer be a reality for you. You are getting there – do not be disheartened. Hummingbird energy will take you further along the path to liberation if you invite it into your life now and ask it to accompany you on your journey. There is no doubt that this journey is getting somewhere, and that all your good work is slowly lifting you out of the mire of illusion into the light of Truth.

If you relate strongly to the hummingbird as your own bird symbol, then you are using the power of the hummingbird in your own life, to lift yourself out of pain and suffering, and almost certainly to help others do the same as well. You understand quite naturally how to do this. There is a glow about you that reminds people of joyful things just by being around you.

The hum of the hummingbird's wings is the OM of existence. Joy lives in that vibration, and peace, and love. You have drawn this card today to signal that your time of suffering is drawing to a close and that truly you can expect magic and wonderment to fill your days.

33   SUNBIRD   **33**

Affirmation

'I ask the overlighting consciousness of the sunbird to light up my day. I know that I am blessed, and that abundance and companionship are mine to enjoy. I acknowledge my contribution to this world, and allow in the offerings that life is sending me in return. I choose to have fun now.'

Sunbird

Sunbirds are the most beautiful, iridescent jewels, that make us rejoice in the sheer beauty and wonder of the natural world. These exquisite little nectar-seekers carry the precious energy of abundance. They speak to us of the richness of our lives and remind us of the fact that there is a bountiful nature that supports and nourishes us with its sweet offerings. Sunbirds fly in pairs, and remind us also of the joy of a shared passage through life. A sunbird in your garden is like a precious little jewel, sent by God to remind you that the abundance of the universe is yours to enjoy.

If you are a sunbird by nature then you evoke a joyful response from life. Relationships are important to you and you attract many who want to be your friend. You tend to be quite choosy about whom you allow close to you, and will prefer to be in the company of just one or two special companions, although you are a great team person when you have to be, because of your lovely sense of fun. If you are a sunbird, you will be blessed with the joy of a truly compatible marriage. God smiles on sunbirds, and this is one of the gifts of life that is yours to cherish. The other gift of life that is bestowed on these precious people, is the ability to attract material prosperity to themselves. They always can be sure of the material support of the universe. This is because they are offering so much to life in return. Their presence on the planet brings such joy and richness to so many people's lives.

Sunbird people know in their hearts that their mate is destined to show up in their lives at exactly the right moment. However many apparently wonderful people may clamour for their hand in marriage, they are blessed with an inner tuning fork that resonates only to the sound of that one person who will fulfil their longing for a soul companion.

If you have chosen the sunbird card today, then it is a day of rich reward. Know that life is promising sweet blessings. You have given to life, and the rich harvest has begun. God is smiling upon you and sending you gifts. You will not lack for true soul friendships, nor for material advantages. Life is saying thank you; you are a precious asset to this world, and your contributions have not gone unnoticed. Have fun now and enjoy the nectar of life.

34 VULTURE **34**

Affirmation

'I ask the overlighting consciousness of the vulture to assist me in forgiving this shameful aspect of myself that I am facing at the moment. Help me to recognise my value as a person despite what I am seeing right now. I know that I am loved; that I am a Divine being having a human experience; that I am always whole and that this experience of shame is an illusion. Especially I know that by acknowledging and forgiving this shame I move closer to my perfect Self.'

Vulture

Vultures can transmute that which is sordid into life-giving nourishment for themselves. Behind their grotesque appearance, and blood-curdling activities, lies a precious gift. Both on the physical level, and in terms of what is offered by the overlighting consciousness of the vulture, the gift is the ability to take something that is putrefying, consume it, and thereby transform it back into a constructive part of the life-cycle again.

You are unlikely to be drawn to the vulture as your own special symbol. But if you are, or if a vulture has made an unexpected appearance in your life in some way, then there is a dark, shameful side of your life that you are trying to bring into the light to be cleansed and forgiven. Just as the vulture needs to be appreciated for the gift that it offers, this shadow side of yourself is asking to be examined closely. You do need to face it and see its loathsome aspects fully too, but then ask how this shadow side has served you. Once you have perceived its gift, it will be easier to forgive and bless that part of yourself that you would rather had remained hidden.

Similarly, if you have drawn the vulture card today, life is offering you the gift of the overlighting consciousness of the vulture, to help you to face and forgive a part of your nature that you find hard to accept. We all have our shadow side. While this shadow side remains hidden and unexamined, it exerts enormous power over us, causing us to do things we hate in ourselves. Once we have owned these unredeemed aspects of ourselves, and faced them consciously, their power can become constructive, rather than destructive. This is where vulture energy can assist very deeply. It knows exactly how to shift destructive, shadow energy into constructive, love energy.

Your card is suggesting that you invite this energy into your life to help you to move through this difficult process of facing all your secret shames, and coming at last to a place where you know that, despite all of your sins, you are a lovable, beautiful, whole, and totally worthwhile, human being.

35   PHEASANT   **35**

Affirmation

'I am one with my true Self. I joyously celebrate my true nature, which is God. I see my attributes and glory in them. I am a majestically beautiful being.'

Pheasant

Pheasants are royalty in the bird kingdom. Royal blood confers power and authority – and this is what the pheasant energy radiates. However, this is not expressed in a bombastic way. The kind of power and authority expressed by the overlighting consciousness of the pheasant is the power and authority to shift consciousness momentously; perhaps even from one dimension to another.

You have drawn the pheasant card today because pheasant energy commands that you take note that your ascension process is well under way. You are connecting with your own power and authority now. The shadow aspect of your nature has been harnessed; it no longer undermines your progression towards a full connection with your own source of power. Rather, you are triumphantly making use of the golden shadow – those beautiful aspects of self that up until now you have not acknowledged, or fully utilised. Look at the glowing beauty of the majestic pheasant and know that this glorious plumage is a reflection of who you really are. These are your true colours. Can you not love something so exquisitely beautiful?

If the pheasant has been a recurring symbol in your life, then the overlighting consciousness of the pheasant has been working with you, to help you to engage with your own power source, and to move you along your path to full ascension. You can actively invite it into your process and work consciously with it to rise above the hurdles that you encounter along the way. There will be powerful moments of initiation, where your consciousness shifts radically to higher levels of perception and wisdom. This is where pheasant consciousness has the necessary specific kind of dynamic energy that can push through into new awareness.

Huge forces have been working through you, but now you have come to a place of equilibrium, where you can stop a moment and take stock. Look at yourself, as if looking in a mirror. Sense the nobility of your bearing. Feel the spiritual authority that you can command. Know that your soul emanates the most glorious array of gold and iridescent colours. Notice the love pouring from your heart. And then, love this person that you see – because what you are seeing is Self, which is God.

36   TURKEY   **36**

Affirmation

'I thank all the magnificent beings and people who have helped me reach this place. I revel in my sense of achievement. I love myself for listening to my own dream. I allow the overlighting consciousness of the turkey to flood my heart with gratitude for life's grace.'

Turkey

36

Turkey energy helps us express the spirit of gratitude. Turkeys are ridiculous-looking creatures, but they carry a strong heart energy, of love and goodwill. The overlighting consciousness of the turkey is actually a great being, which offers up its creatures in a spirit of openhearted service to humanity. Death is not an issue in the bird kingdom. The spirit of the turkey expresses itself again and again, through form and then effortlessly out of form. It is not death that is the problem; it is whether or not the spirit of the turkey is honoured in the process. Those that remember to thank the spirit of the turkey which they are about to consume, receive the nourishment not only of its body, but also of its loving heart.

If you have chosen the turkey card today, then thanksgiving is the focus of life's message to you. You have just arrived somewhere – physically or metaphorically – and you need to stop for a moment, and reflect on all the assistance that life has offered you to get you to where you are now. You have been given so much rich support and guidance. There are so many beautiful beings and people who deserve your heartfelt gratitude. There is so much love for you from them all.

And then, thank your own beautiful Self. Honour yourself for your perseverance and commitment to your own truth. Remind yourself of the many battles you have fought along the way to arrive at this place. It takes a great deal of trust to follow your heart's song; thank yourself for trusting life enough to listen to, and to act upon, your inner knowing. Step by step, it has brought you to this place.

People for whom the turkey has special significance are offering their lives in sacrificial service to a greater cause. Their joy is in knowing that, although they are not individually acknowledged, they are part of a community that is heard in the world.

Savour this satisfying feeling of having arrived somewhere. There is never an end to the possibilities of growth and exploration, so this is not where you will stay for ever. But, for now, it's great to have landed!

37 LOVEBIRD **37**

Affirmation

'I ask for the help of the overlighting consciousness of the lovebird to break open my heart. Reveal to me what the most loving action is for me to follow right now. Be with me as I step into true Love. I honour my beloved.'

Lovebird

37

Lovebird energy has an intense impact upon the heart chakra. It softens and opens the heart so that more loving energy can flow through. The overlighting consciousness of the lovebird expresses the Archangel Michael's divinely authorised mission on this planet; to hold the forcefield of love so that each creature and element upon this earth can lift up through the density and heaviness of physical existence into the Light of Spirit. Lovebirds are part of the matrix of life that holds this forcefield in place for us.

You have drawn the lovebird card today because you are going through an initiation of the heart. You are blasting through to a new and more powerful expression of love. When your heart opens up, you know your connectedness with every level of existence in the universe. You can never feel alone again. Eventually, you will have a full experience of total oneness with God; this is a big step in that direction.

If the lovebird has been a favourite symbol for you, then God is very present in your life. You are already allowing a powerful flow of love energy through your heart. Many people benefit from the impact this has on them – you are a much-loved person yourself as a result.

The energy of the lovebird is an expression of the beautiful unconditional love that can exist between two soulmates. The attraction of soulmates for one another is extremely powerful and can transcend many apparent cultural or man-made obstacles – such as age, religion, race or sex. The soul wants to bring the two parts of itself together, and the two people involved feel the tremendous yearning to implode into oneness. However, part of the challenge of a soulmate relationship is to love the beloved so unconditionally that one truly wants only that which serves him or her the most – and sometimes physical union is not appropriate. It is the greatest gift one can ever give another soul – to love that person so unconditionally that one can discern when it is appropriate to claim the beloved one for oneself, or when it is more appropriate to let go and slip away.

PHOENIX

38   38

Affirmation

'I ask the overlighting consciousness of the phoenix to assist me to transcend the destruction of the structures that were my support before. Help me to recognise the greater freedom I move towards. I joyously step into my new life, knowing that I will not regret what I leave behind.'

Phoenix

38

The mythical phoenix has a magnificent consciousness associated with it; although it does not exist on the physical plane, it has form on more subtle dimensions, where its rarefied energy is more appropriate.

You have drawn the phoenix card today because you are needing to use this magnificent being's energy to rise up out of a calamity and turn it into a personal triumph. Something is happening which appears to be the collapse of your known structures. This is the moment to draw on your own treasures and turn the apparent disaster into a situation which allows you to transcend the mess. Phoenix energy is available to help you to do this. The phoenix rises up out of the ashes of destruction into glorious flight. You can do this too.

The phoenix is a very potent symbol to have as a personal favourite – it implies that you have had much practice in flying free of the ruins of old structures. You know in your heart that you can transcend any apparent limitation. You therefore do not allow yourself to become too attached to the form of things.

You need to accept that something is about to change form. You are being alerted to this through the phoenix card today. Remember that you as a soul can never be destroyed. Destruction is simply an illusion – the physical form of things changes, but the spirit behind all things is eternal. You are eternal – you change your form, but the essential *you* cannot be changed. What is it that is asking to be broken down so that the spirit can be released? When the spirit behind the form is needing to move beyond its present limitations, it will create a situation where the form collapses, and the spirit rises again triumphantly from the ruins of the old, in order to start a new life. The new life is always moving closer to God – there is always greater freedom and more joy when the soul moves on. Never fear change – it is the soul demanding a new form to express itself through, and it is always moving you further into Love.

CUCKOO

39 **39**

Affirmation

'I thank the overlighting consciousness of the cuckoo for signalling the start of a new cycle. I greet my future with excited expectation.'

Cuckoo

The cuckoo calls us to new life. Its beautiful wake-up call reverberates through the Alps in spring-time, and its voice is heard in many other parts of the world as well.

When you draw the cuckoo card, know that a new life is dawning for you. There is spring in the air – let the anticipation of a glorious summer put joy in your heart and a skip in your step. It is time to start a new cycle. Put the old behind you – you are moving towards joy now.

If the cuckoo is a favourite symbol of yours, then you are a person who is aware of many blessings in your life. You anticipate that good things will come your way, and allow yourself to constantly refresh yourself with new ways of doing things. You do not allow yourself to get stuck in old patterns for too long. The urge to spring-clean is too strong in you!

You may have drawn the cuckoo card today because you need the help of the overlighting consciousness of the cuckoo to move out of an old rut and into a new rush of creative energy. If you feel this way, it often helps to do a thorough clean-up of your physical space. Throw out all unnecessary junk and freshen up your environment. Do some emotional cleansing also – release all hostility and pent-up resentment by allowing the energy of compassion to flow through your heart. This releases stuck energy to be used creatively in your own life.

The cuckoo calls us to new beginnings – step into your future with clear intentions and intense anticipation.

40   WARBLER   **40**

Affirmation

'I ask the overlighting consciousness of the warbler to be my companion in my current situation. I ask God to show me what to do to unblock my throat and allow my truth to pour forth unrestrainedly.'

Warbler

The warbler sings its song of joy with beautiful abandon. There is no sense of constraint here. The liquid sound pours from its throat in a wonderful stream of expressive trilling. The gift that the warbler offers is a healing energy which can be used to break through problems in self-expression. People who find it difficult to put across their ideas, or who are blocked in any way in the throat chakra, can use the warbler energy with great effect.

You have drawn the warbler card today because you need assistance in the area of self-expression. It may be that you are in a situation where you are struggling to speak your truth and be heard. Many people find public speaking absolutely terrifying. You may be facing such a prospect in the near future and need help to unblock the fear sitting in your throat chakra. Perhaps you are a person who never speaks up for yourself when you find yourself in an uncomfortable situation. Whatever the individual problem is, the overlighting consciousness of the warbler can be called upon to help you move through your fear and unblock the constraint in the throat chakra.

Conversely, if you are someone who chooses the warbler easily as a special symbol for yourself, then self-expression is one of your great strengths. You have mastered the art of holding an audience's attention in public speaking, and you have no problem demanding your rights, very vociferously if necessary. Your voice is a wonderful tool, which you use to your advantage. The warbler's energy can work in your life with no resistance at all.

The throat chakra, which is the area through which you speak your truth, needs to be gradually brought into alignment with the heart chakra, so that you speak your truth with love, and not with arrogance, or contempt for those you address. Once this alignment has taken place, both the heart and the throat can be brought into alignment with the crown chakra, so that when you speak you are expressing the truth of your own Self, which is one with God. The warbler pours forth pure love, which is pure Spirit, and its overlighting consciousness can be called upon to help you to bring your heart, throat and crown into complete alignment with God.

41 ROLLER **41**

Affirmation

'I invite the overlighting consciousness of the roller to remind me of who I really AM.'

Roller

Rollers are the physical expression on earth of an overlighting consciousness which is very attuned to the highest spiritual dimensions. They are exquisite little birds, with beautiful lilac, turquoise, green and blue, in various combinations, in the plumage of the different species. These high-frequency colours reflect their resonance with very subtle dimensions of consciousness.

The gift of the roller consciousness is that it brings one back to the conscious recognition of the simple truth of our existence – that we and God are One – always. The illusion is that we are separate and are slowly moving back toward God. The truth is that we have never been anywhere but with God. God is in every breath we take, every morsel of food we eat, and in every atom and molecule of every cell in our bodies. We cannot be separate from God because we *are* God, in our physical make-up and in our souls. The game of life is to remember this. We struggle and pray and weep for our sins and think that God could not possibly love us – and it is very real, and very painful while we are in it. But there comes a moment when an inner shift takes place, and suddenly it dawns on us that we knew another truth once.

This is the gift of the overlighting consciousness of the roller – to remind us. There is always a timing to this inner shift, and it often comes when we are least expecting it. If you have drawn the roller card today, then life is putting you on alert that you and God are about to get reacquainted!

If rollers have always been a favourite bird symbol for you, then you know who you are already. You are like a lighthouse in the dark for those who have lost their way – without having to say a word, the fact that you have remembered ignites an answering light in their own souls, which will lead them to the truth of their oneness with God, in their own perfect timing.

42 ORIOLE **42**

Affirmation

'I invite the overlighting consciousness of the oriole to be my companion over these difficult days, to give me the inner strength and courage to move forward. I know that I have the inner resources to do what I have to do and that God is with me on this journey.'

Oriole

The oriole is a happy-go-lucky songster, with a predominance of yellow in its plumage. The yellow gives the clue to the energy that this bird consciousness makes available. Like the yellow canary, the yellow oriole offers us a lift – a burst of sunshine and happy sound that can lift us out of our doldrums, and back into harmony with life again.

If you have drawn the oriole card today, then you are tired somewhere deep in your soul. You have been carrying a burden for too long, and your soul longs for a respite. Oriole energy is just what you need to heal this sense of not being able to go another step. Use it very consciously – ask the overlighting consciousness of the oriole to be with you; to nourish you while you sleep, and to be your companion in the days to come. It is a wonderfully energising companion. You will go that extra mile.

If orioles have been your own favourite bird symbol, then you yourself are a tonic to those around you. Be aware that your presence can be a powerful boost to someone who is feeling low. You just have to be there, not even necessarily physically – the telephone is also a wonderful transmitter of energy between two people. Don't underestimate the difference you can make in a person's life just by making that energy connection at a crucial moment.

We all need the sun. Yellow is sun energy and it is a colour that can be used very effectively to heal despondency. Breathe it in, and imagine that your body slowly fills up and becomes saturated with yellow. Hold the colour in your body until you feel yourself coming into balance. At this point, invite the over-lighting consciousness of the oriole to assist you to continue on your journey.

43   WEAVER   **43**

Affirmation
'I invite the overlighting consciousness of the weaver to be my companion as I search for my true home.'

Weaver

The weaver's energy gives form to the impulse we all have to make a home base for ourselves. The overlighting consciousness of the weaver can offer real practical assistance if called upon to help during a process of establishing a home.

You have drawn the weaver card today because, whatever this might mean to you individually, your home base is calling for your attention. Do you know where 'home' is? Is it a physical dwelling, or is it a resting place within your soul? It can be both – for many people the inner resting place is more easily accessed within the physical home space. Are you having difficulty finding this sense of coming home to yourself? The fact that you have drawn this card suggests that you are. You may be having difficulty on a practical physical level with establishing your home, but this is very likely reflecting that you are not sitting comfortably in your own inner world either. This is where the energy of the weaver bird can help – both physically and on an inner level, to help you establish that sense of home base.

The weaver bird establishes its home within a community. Everyone is part of a community. When you were created, you were created as an individual soul within a family of souls. This is your true family and your own personal community. However, the connection with your own family may not be possible on an outer physical level – they may be elsewhere on the planet, or not incarnated in physical bodies. Therefore, your ultimate community is something you connect with on an inner level. This is part of what is meant by coming 'home'. You are loved and recognised by your own family, and somewhere on your own spiritual journey you will find them, whether on the outer or the inner level. The overlighting consciousness of the weaver can be asked to be your own personal assistant in the process of coming home to your own soul community. It is a big step in the journey toward truly knowing who you are.

44 PARTRIDGE 44

Affirmation

'I ask the overlighting consciousness of the partridge to help me to allow God's love to enter my soul.'

Partridge

Partridges, francolins, guinea fowl and other ground birds offer a very similar energy with basically the same message. They invite us to join the humble legion of God's creatures who know that, despite their inability to rise very far off the ground, they are truly loved.

You have drawn the partridge card today to remind you that it is only human beings who take themselves so seriously that they feel unable to see themselves as worthy of God's love. Every other living creature just allows itself to bask in the warmth of God's loving embrace, but as a human being you do not allow this loving embrace to flow through your body and soul as an automatic event. You block the flow because of a myriad different guilts and self-judgements. The partridge card is an invitation to allow God's love and acceptance to flow through you and heal your aching heart. Only you can make this choice.

God is ready to forgive in an instant – you have to forgive yourself first. This is the most difficult thing for any human being – to allow that what you see as your own terrible sin and shame is never too great to be forgiven by God – as long as you can forgive it in yourself. Sometimes forgiving it in another is the key to being able to forgive it in yourself – that is why so often we draw people into our lives who reflect our exact secret shames. We often hate those people, because we do not recognise our own darker selves in their more obvious actions. The key is forgiveness, because once you have given compassion and acceptance to someone outside of yourself, you are more able to forgive that within your own being.

If you have always had a partridge or similar bird as your own favourite symbol, then you are already one of those humble creatures who know they are truly loved despite all their clumsiness and apparent lack of elegance. You can help others to gain a greater level of self-acceptance because of your own unselfconscious self-love. The overlighting consciousness of the partridge is always available to help anyone struggling with a lack of self-acceptance. Ask, and you will start to feel the response of God's ever-present love.

45 WAGTAIL **45**

Affirmation

'I invite the overlighting consciousness of the wagtail to be present in my life. I acknowledge that I need cheering up!'

Wagtail

Wagtails bring cheer into a situation. The little wagtail, with its bobbing rear end, immediately lifts the vibration of its environment – one cannot help smiling at this little cheerful creature.

When a wagtail drops into your life for a moment, stop what you are doing and focus on its energy. If you allow its energy to wash over you, you will experience a lift of the spirit. This is what the energy of the wagtail card offers you as well – it comes into your life to give you a lift. You may be in a crisis, or simply feeling depressed, and the energy of the wagtail is perfect for you. You need to look outside yourself and allow life to give you a boost. Then you can go back into your situation revitalised and with new perspective.

If you have always related to the wagtail as your own special bird, then you yourself are one of those gifted human beings who quite naturally lift a situation into good humour with your presence. This is a wonderful characteristic, and always much appreciated by the more melancholic members of the human family.

The overlighting presence of the wagtail is a real source of cheer that you can tap into at the moment. You are needing this energy – this is why you have chosen the card. So take a moment to ask the overlighting consciousness of the wagtail to give you the lift you need to cope with your present situation – there will be a real response.

46   RAVEN   **46**

Affirmation

'I ask the overlighting consciousness of the raven to show me God's purpose for me. I know that whatever change is coming is Love's way of bringing me closer to the ultimate marriage – of Self with God.'

Raven

46

Ravens speak to us of change and transmutation. This can sometimes mean a death but, as with the owl, this death does not necessarily mean a physical parting but rather the end of one kind of life, and the beginning of another. Ravens are not messengers of anything sinister – they are powerful transmitters of God's Holy Word.

If you have drawn the raven card now, God is transmitting a powerful message to you. The essence of the message is: 'Beloved, I greet you as my child. I want you to see Me now. I therefore draw the veils aside so that you may break through the illusion of separation, and see My face. I am Love. I am coming.'

If the raven has always been a powerful bird in your life, then perhaps you are also an instrument for God's Word. Perhaps you are also able to transmit this message of Love to those whom God is calling.

47   GANNET   **47**

Affirmation

'I thank God for the blessings being offered to me today. I ready myself to receive all of them. There is *no* limit to the number of blessings I am prepared to open myself to enjoy.'

Gannet

The gannet is a seabird, like the cormorant, and in our language is associated with greed – a gannet is also the term for a greedy person. The overlighting consciousness of the gannet is in fact a very powerful presence, which can be called upon when one is wanting to multiply something in one's life. Whether it be money, love, job opportunities – whatever you are particularly needing to expand for yourself – the energy of the gannet can help you to make it happen.

You have drawn the gannet card today because, whether you are aware of it or not, life is offering you an opportunity to expand something. What do you think you are needing more of at present? Stop and think for a moment. Then ask the overlighting consciousness of the gannet to work with you. Visualise in detail what you are asking for, and hold that visual picture very clearly for as long as you can. Do this whenever you have a spare moment through the day. Do not be afraid to command what you want. It is so often our own sense of not being worthy to receive that blocks the flow of abundance for us. Know that you deserve this – and command life to give it to you!

If you relate to the gannet as a powerful symbol for yourself, then you have the potential to use the positive expression of this bird's energy to create abundant quantities of whatever is important in your life. Use this powerful bird's magnifying qualities with discernment!

You have chosen the gannet card today because there is a flow of beneficent universal energy in your direction. You can choose to allow it to work fully in your favour, or you can block the blessings it brings you through your own unwillingness to receive. Your Self wants you to have everything the universe can give you. Can you allow yourself to be big enough to receive all of life?

48 SHRIKE **48**

Affirmation

'I ask the overlighting consciousness of the shrike to be present as I break through this situation to a higher expression of life. I ask God to guide the process to harmonious resolution.'

Shrike

Shrike energy is harsh and formidable. The 'butcher bird' (fiscal shrike), which impales its prey on thorns and barbed wire, is an accurate expression of what this energy feels like.

You have chosen the shrike card today in answer to a question, or as a daily reading, because you are needing shrike energy to be absolutely callous and ruthless in some area of your life. Sometimes shrike energy is necessary to get something done, or to remove somebody who is jamming up a process that needs to move forward. Here you need clarity, and intent, and absolute trust in your own power to create good. You use this shrike energy with the inner awareness that only that which brings forth the highest good for all concerned will manifest as a result.

Shrike energy often manifests with anger. You can use anger to break through a logjam situation, but it must be righteous anger. You must be coming from your own truth, not use blame or diminish the person's worth. If you use the anger like a sword, to cut through all the verbiage that is obscuring the real issue – then you will be using shrike energy in a very healing and constructive way. It is easy to get caught up in the emotion of the anger, and then you lose its potential for lifting the situation to a higher level. If you call upon the over-lighting consciousness of the shrike to be with you when you strike, you will find that the rapier thrust of the anger is absolutely effective and that you can distance yourself from the turbulence the anger produces in you.

If you have related to the shrike as your own bird symbol, then you are a powerful force to contend with. Always align yourself with your highest good when you use the shrike type of energy, otherwise the potential destructive impact of its ruthlessness may become too strong. Stand in your own truth, align yourself with God, and then you can cut through old forms with wonderfully uplifting effect.

(49) WREN **(49)**

Affirmation

'I invite the overlighting consciousness of the wren to work with me to erase old outmoded thinking from my body cells. I now choose to believe that joy, prosperity, health, happiness and love are mine for the taking, and that everything always works out perfectly.'

Wren

49

The wren is a pretty little bird. It evokes a tender response from its onlookers – its presence is a delight and brings a lift of the heart, rather like the robin. Its energy feels different from the robin, however; it offers the possibility of rising above the third-dimensional struggle of pain and suffering into a higher-dimensional version of reality, where there is the possibility of only joyous outcomes to all one's endeavours. Here there is perfect peace, permanent happiness and undiluted Love. The little wren carries this resonance, and if you invite the overlighting consciousness of the wren to work with you in your life, you too will be shown ways to lift yourself above the sense of endless struggle, so that you can see the joy that pulsates behind the apparent façade of death and decay.

You have drawn the wren card today specifically to bring you to an awareness that you need to change your expectation of your life. You are carrying a belief inside you that says that life has to be difficult. It says that the possibility that things will turn out happily for you is very slim. The chances are things will go wrong. Do you realise that until you consciously change this deeply rooted belief, this is exactly how it will be for you? Each person individually has to rise up out of this mass hypnosis and see for him or her self the direct connection between this belief and the reality that is expressing itself in his or her life.

Once you see the connection and realise your own individual responsibility to choose something different, things will change immeasurably for you. Take your thoughts and deep subconscious beliefs into your conscious control. Subdue all negative statements as they arise. Use meditation programmes to learn to connect with your inner being – and then learn to reprogram yourself with a new possibility. There is a reality out there that responds to the absolute confidence that only joyous outcomes will express themselves in your life. Once you believe it, it will be your reality.

The overlighting consciousness of the wren is a reminder to us of this possibility of joyous outcomes. It carries this absolute confidence in its little bird form. If you tune into this consciousness it will be an enormous help in bringing you to your own absolute knowledge that only joyous outcomes are possible for you from now on.

50 **OSTRICH** **50**

Affirmation
'I see my ostrich self and I see the light that surrounds it. I ask the overlighting consciousness of the ostrich to help me to expand my vision to go beyond the opposites to truly know in every cell of my body that *there is only light.*'

Ostrich

50

The ostrich is known for its head-in-the-sand refusal to look at what is happening all around it. The ostrich is also known for the fact that it doesn't know how to fly. The overlighting energy of the ostrich is there for those people who need the protection of their own comforting reality prison, and who really don't want to know that there is blue sky and light beyond their prison bars. Before you laughingly dismiss yourself from this category, ask yourself this question: 'Do you believe that *there is only light?*' The answer, if you are honest, will surprise you. You see, the truth is, there *is* only light. You are that light, and so is absolutely everything else. There is no particle or sub-, micro-particle that is not light. The light of God is everywhere. Darkness is the apparent absence of light – but if every single particle in that darkness is also God, how can it not be light? So, you see, *there is only light.*

If you have taken the ostrich card today, then you are being asked to look seriously at this statement. The ostrich sticks its head in the sand and will not look at the obvious fact that sand is not actually the reality that envelops it. Light is. Please take your head out of the sand for a moment and look around. There is a much more exciting environment to encompass than just sand. You are limiting your viewpoint – let your vision open up!

If the ostrich has always been a favourite symbol for you, then it does not necessarily mean that you are an incredibly tunnel-visioned person! What it could mean is that you are working quite deeply with the lesson the ostrich energy works with. This is to go beyond the opposites – the light and the dark – and to realise in every cell of your body that beyond these opposites there truly is only one God – Light – in which one finds resolution of the paradox of these opposites. Within that resolution are bliss, joy, love. To know that *there is only light* is to know ultimate release from the necessity of knowing darkness.

51 NIGHTJAR **51**

Affirmation

'I am ready to face my worst fears. I ask the overlighting consciousness of the nightjar to help me to bring them up to consciousness, and I will master them.'

Nightjar

Nightjar energy comes out of the dark. In the daylight our fears and anxieties can often be suppressed or ignored, but at night, in the dark, they rise up to confront us, sometimes seeming very big and monstrous and keeping us awake. The overlighting consciousness of the nightjar works to bring our deepest fears up into our conscious awareness, so making it possible to face and master them.

You have drawn the nightjar card today because a deep fear is surfacing in you. You are probably already trying to deal with it. The card is suggesting that you need help. You may need actual therapy – and there is no shame in that – or at least an understanding person to share your fear with. Do not blame yourself for being unable to rationalise the fear away. A huge fear like this is totally undeterred by conscious rationalisation. It is just too huge in you right now.

The first step is to name it. Find the exact description of the fear. Repeat the name of the fear and feel where it resides in your body. As you name it, you may feel that place in your body move to another place – and then the name of the fear might change to another, slightly different fear. Continue with this process – naming the fear and following it in your body – until you find the place in your body where the energy naturally calms down.

You will probably have to do this many, many times, but each time you do it, you feel a little more strongly that *you* are not the fear. The fear is something that has you in its grip, but you are in fact outside that fear, trying to name it. The second step is to find the core event that caused the fear in the first place. You will probably need some expert help here. There are many wonderful types of therapy available now that can access the core event and help you to clear its energy from your body cells so that you no longer hold it in your reality. The nightjar is a catalyst for bringing you to an awareness of your deep fears. If you are already in a very supportive framework of therapy, and confident in your ability to face and master your worst fears, then call on the overlighting consciousness of the nightjar to help you to bring them up to the surface for release. It will speed up your process and facilitate complete clearing. It is a wonderful space to be in, to have faced and mastered your worst fears. Nothing can hold you back from allowing the magnificence of who you really are to express itself through you. So, when you are ready, call on the nightjar and dance into the light!

52 WOODPECKER **52**

Affirmation

'I need to move forward with … I invite the overlighting consciousness of the woodpecker to be at my side until I reach my goal. I also invite my Divine Self to reveal to me whether or not this goal is in the best interests of my highest purpose – and if not, to show me a better goal.'

Woodpecker

The woodpecker carries a very solid vibration. In other words, the energy is able to impact quite forcibly on physical matter. The woodpecker's ability to chop away patiently at the wood of the tree, until it makes a hole for its nest, provides the picture that shows us how strong this energy is.

You have chosen the woodpecker card today, in answer to a question, or as a daily reading, because you are needing an energy that will persistently and unremittingly work with you towards a desired goal. What are you trying to achieve in your life at present? Are you trying to push through to a particular desired outcome? A goal weight, for example, or a study program? Anything that needs focus, willpower and dedication, could do with help from the over-lighting consciousness of the woodpecker. It most certainly helps you to stay on course. The crest on the head of some types of woodpecker is an indication that the woodpecker also helps you to align with the will of your Self – so that what you achieve is an expression of your Divine nature.

If the woodpecker has been a favourite bird symbol of yours, then you yourself are a dedicated hard worker, who probably has already notched up quite a few achievements in the physical world. This is a wonderful quality to have, but it is even more powerful if the energy is used in harness with Divine Will.

As with everything in life, your goal will be achieved more easily if you set your intention very clearly at the beginning. Invite in the overlighting conscious-ness of the woodpecker, and then state very clearly, in detail, what it is that you wish to have achieved by the end of the process. Thank it for its help, and proceed!

ROOTER

53   ROOSTER   53

Affirmation

'I am the champion of the world! I ask the overlighting consciousness of the rooster to help me crow today.'

Rooster

Rooster energy is the cocky, triumphant crow of someone who feels master of the universe! The rooster knows he is king of the world, and wakes everyone up to tell them so. Rooster energy is definitely not subtle, nor is it the least bit deprecating. It wants everyone to know that it is the most magnificent bird in the history of the world!

You have chosen the rooster card today because you need to allow yourself to crow with triumphant joy. Allow yourself a moment of sheer undiluted celebration. You have climbed a mountain, and you are the king of the castle. Don't miss your opportunity to do a little cock-a-doodle-dooing! Let rip. The world can do with a bit of sheer exultant joy energy. It does her heart good.

The hen, on the other hand, is a rather more restrained creature, in contrast to her strutting mate. Hen energy is the energy of 'putting up with'. It is the positive aspect of this energy that allows the poor hen to survive the terrible abuse of commercial chicken farming. She just 'puts up with' everything that life throws at her.

Most of us are in hen mode most of our lives. We 'put up with' all manner of undignified situations and joyless restricted realities. We need that patient, uncomplaining hen energy to get through our daily circumscribed routines. But every now and again, something happens which allows us to break through that sense of drudgery, and feel undiluted, unrestricted, glorious, victorious, cockerel-crowing, triumph. When that happens – give it all you've got!

If the rooster is your favourite bird symbol, then crowing is something you do well! You find the time to break out into triumphal rejoicing at the magnificence of who you really are. And you are magnificent – we should all be waking up every morning with that unabashed rooster energy: 'Good morning, wonderful day – look at magnificent me – here in all my glory for you to shine your light upon – I AM THE CHAMPION OF THE WORLD'. Start your day like that, and see how life jumps to your command!

54 DODO **54**

Affirmation

'I invite the overlighting consciousness of the dodo to work with me to release all that is old and stagnant in my energy system (or, to work with me to release this person who has come to me for help). I ask that a higher expression of Self be able to express itself through me (or, this person) as a result.'

Dodo

54

The dodo is a strange bird to include – because it is extinct – but its energy can still be tapped into. No creature that has existed on earth is ever truly extinct. Its physical body may not be available here any longer, but its consciousness can never be destroyed. The physical body simply reflects the presence on earth of a being whose consciousness may express itself in other realities through other forms.

You have chosen the dodo card today because something in you is choosing to move on. There is some belief, some old tired format, that does not serve you any longer. It is keeping you stuck in a particular way of seeing things. Often we don't realise that we are manifesting certain things in our current reality because we still believe things that our parents believed, and their parents before them. Really important things, like 'I can never be a success', or 'No-one will ever truly love me'. If you seem to be up against a wall in some area of your life, you are most likely bashing your head against one of these beliefs. Look at what the lack in your life is saying about what you must believe – and then set about reprogramming yourself with a new, more expansive belief.

This is where the energy of the dodo can be tapped into. Invite the overlighting consciousness of the dodo to help you to release the outmoded belief, to make room for the new one. Dodo energy is finer than you might expect, considering that it was a flightless bird that was part of an older era. It has a very strong cauterising quality, which works to cut you off from old energy that has held you captive.

If you have always regarded the dodo as a favourite bird symbol, then it is possible that you work as an energy healer, or bodyworker, specifically working to help people release programming that is keeping them stuck – and dodo energy is what you are working with, without realising it. If you make this a more conscious partnership, you will find that your clearing work can be even more finely executed. Invite the overlighting consciousness of the dodo to work with you, and feel how this beautiful consciousness reaches into the situation and draws out that which needs to go.

BLUE BIRD OF HAPPINESS

55   55

Affirmation

'There is no reason for me to fear joy. Joy is who I AM. I ask the overlighting consciousness of the bird kingdom to fill me with the forgotten joy. Help me to move from understanding that I am perfect, to knowing that I AM. Help me to remember that there is nothing that needs to be changed or mended, because I AM already Whole, and always have been.'

Blue Bird of Happiness

The blue bird of happiness is not a physical specimen – it is an experience within the heart. It is that little bubble of joy that bursts through and explodes one into laughter and love. It is our own soul breaking through the personality and reminding us that we are entitled to joy.

If you have taken this card today, then there is a bubble of happiness trying to make itself felt through the loneliness and isolation. Allow it to burst forth, and just feel *happy*. Happiness is a great healer. The energy of happiness fills your cells with healing vibrations. Just allow yourself to feel happy. This little blue bird is just a symbol, but it does represent the place in your heart that knows joy. We all have a place of joy, even if we very seldom access it. It is the place in our hearts where we know God. As human beings we are at our most unhappy place when we feel cut off from Spirit. We cut ourselves off, and then wonder why we feel so lost and lonely. Spirit is joy – and love, and happiness.

This little blue bird really represents the essence of what the bird kingdom as a whole offers us as a human family. We all know the lift of the heart that the arrival of a bird – any bird – can give us when we are feeling down. The birds carry different vibrations, but essentially they bear the same message: 'We are all One. You are a part of me. I come to you as a part of your Self, bringing the reminder that the essence of who you are is God. You are a magnificent being, made in the image of God. You experience yourself as separate from God, but we are like the angels – we know that there is no separation and that God simply *is* in us. Our presence in your lives is God's blessing to this planet, to keep the possibility of joy and love and peace alive here, until you realise that you *are* it.'

The Artist's Notes

The original drawings are made in A5 size, and I used the excellent colour pencils of Berol Karisma, and sometimes white paint for the highlights (for instance, like the little lightspot that makes the eyes shine).

Rainbows are for me personally always a sign of loving positivity; a sign or omen of something very beautiful, or an indication of a special event. (Author's note: When I was driving to the airport to catch the plane to go to Austria to the international event where I would be put in touch with Joyce, there was a rainbow with the most intense colours I have ever experienced, stretching from one side of the sky to the other, and we had to drive 'under' it to the airport. The first card that Joyce illustrated for me, as a sample, was of a kingfisher, encircled by a rainbow. I explained in the Introduction why the choice of the kingfisher was so meaningful to me, but the rainbow also felt highly significant).

1   Pigeon
I placed the pigeon on a bowl made of jade (protection, purification, harmonisation) and amethyst (higher consciousness), and depicted it holding a stick of burning incense in its beak and also with incense burning in the bowl, to indicate the pigeon's function of purifying the environment.

2   Swallow
Soft rainbow colours all over symbolise joy; the rainbow ribbon leads the way, as a symbol of the joyful path to the Light.

3   Robin
The robin holds a diamond heart in its beak, as a symbol of the purest love, which is Divine Love. Roses are of course a symbol of love, and the pink, fully-opened rose portrays the full flowering of the heart chakra.

4 Hawk
The lightning is used as a symbol for a breakthrough. The diamond triangle points upwards, indicating the direction to higher consciousness, and also implies that this energy must be treated with caution, as it is powerful. The hawk sits on a rock where garnet crystals have grown (for energy and perseverance).

5 Dove
The night-sky silhouette of the dove was chosen to show the dove's function in reminding us about our oneness with the universe. I used soft colours for the dove's gentleness, and three diamonds for its power. There are olive branches in the background, for peace.

6 Sparrow
As the symbol for the company of family and friends, I used a 'network' of golden beads behind the birds, and emeralds to convey the atmosphere of harmonious wellbeing.

7 Parrot
The parrot sits high in a tree (has a higher perspective). In the eggshapes are different scenes, as symbols for different points of view. There are closed eggs on the ground, indicating other points of view which have yet to be explored.

8 Thrush
A harmonious green landscape brings peace. The etheric harp shines in the sky and uplifting, heavenly music flows down to the earth, to resonate in anyone who 'wants' to hear it, bringing balance and harmony to the earth.

9 Blackbird
The blackbird is surrounded by a protecting circle of sharp crystal points, but the doors of the inner gate are wide open, where one is welcomed in by the warm, pink light of love.

10 Crow
A green path passes a stone with magical inscriptions (messages from other worlds), and through a gate, leading to a temple where the violet flame of highest wisdom is burning. The crow is the messenger and sits on a curved light-beam that connects our world with higher worlds.

11 Peacock
The all-seeing eye is symbolised in different ways. There are eyes in the piece of malachite, and on the tailfeathers of course, and around the peacock's neck is a jewel with the all-seeing eye of God. There is a path leading to a distant temple, which is a symbol of Self.

12 Swan
On the top of the picture there are images of day and night, in balance, like partners. There is a set of balancing scales with a male/female symbol as the fulcrum, and on the scales are two hearts, each set in a lotus flower, both exactly the same and perfectly in balance, indicating soul partnership. There are two rainbows, coming down from the fulcrum-point to the water, where the swan is swimming. On the horizon is a lit silhouette of a second swan, as a symbol of the perfect partner (and of the inner partner) with whom one has to attain balance.

13 Eagle
The eagle flies with the sun (as a symbol of the power of God) in its claws, high above the earth. Misuse of this power destroys, but correct use of this power has enormous potential for good.

14 Owl
The owl sits on a rainbow as a non-physical border between the mystical and the physical worlds. In the physical world is a lighted path to a dead tree (symbol of old patterns to be released). The golden egg floating in space is a symbol of the not-yet-manifested spiritual forces, that will be birthed out of the egg at the right moment.

15 Stork
The stork can oversee from a very high place how ideas rise from a fertile landscape, and how they become visible in the world.

16 Lark

The lark is rising very determinedly from a place with pain and problems (tornadoes and rain), via a clear, but still-dark sky where there is already a little light (shining stars), to lighter and lighter skies. The 'borders' between these places are rainbows, symbolic of the joy at having reached these points of transition to more light.

17 Nightingale

The nightingale is singing; in the background is the universe (symbol of eternal creation). On the horizon appears, in radiating sunbeams, a 'different' universe – a pink path of Divine Love leads through a gate, to a holy mountain. The lighted tower is the symbol of the home of higher truth, light and love.

18 Ibis

The ibis is in the water, near a temple with a beautiful pink lotus. If the ibis looks at its reflection in the water it sees its real self, symbolised by the sacred ibis, the violet lotus and the violet flames of Divine wisdom.

19 Finch

The stone on which the finch is perched is rhodonite (for inner peace, harmony, brotherhood and service). The rainbows are symbolic of a new cycle – where they connect with the rainbows of others a bright light comes into existence.

20 Canary

The canary sits on a translucent green crystal and is radiating like a sun, from which a lighted path appears. The path is lit by burning amber (symbol of inner vitality and joy), so that it can be followed with full trust.

21 Flamingo

A flamingo stands in a secluded place, not visible to the rest of the group, and is taking the lid off a hidden vessel, from which a powerful rainbow pours. This quiet act, unnoticed by others, is pouring beauty and blessings into the world, to be enjoyed by all.

22 Pelican
The 'letting go' is symbolised here by the letting go of material possessions (the beads), but this is also a metaphor for the letting go of emotional attachments.

23 Kingfisher
The kingfisher sits on a golden-rimmed bowl, on an aquamarine pedestal. There are faceted aquamarine jewels in the gold (aquamarine for deep insight and contact with the Higher Self). The bowl contains all the wisdom of all universes. Under the rock archway we see the endless ocean, which is fed by the high waterfall (the cycle of water being a symbol for eternity).

24 Seagull
The seagull finds a small rock of charoite (transformation and protection) for the healing of unconscious and conscious fears. High in the sky flies an albatross, as a symbol of freedom after healing.

25 Heron
A light-beam is focused through the clouds onto the waterfall, to re-energise and cleanse the water. The light, the candles, the water and the rain all help to purify and cleanse.

26 Duck
The duck with a hostile attitude towards itself is trapped in a grey world, and does not see the beauty of all the colours and aspects of its being, as it would do if it were only to look outside the box of its self-hatred.

27 Penguin
This penguin feels totally trapped in an egg-shaped chain, and does not see that outside the egg-shape there is a soft-coloured aura radiating, which is perfect and full of love. On the top of the picture, a holy lotus flower blooms, as a symbol of the love of God that transcends everything.

28 Plover
The plover stands on a slice of carnelian (for protection and safety). In the background there is danger (dark clouds, eagle, ruined landscape). The plover leaves the carnelian, acts as if it is wounded, and escapes through a small opening to the green, fertile and peaceful world.

29 Goose
As a symbol of 'bountiful blessings', the goose is placed on top of a cave filled with jewels in all colours. In the background is a path leading to a mountain surrounded by clouds, where a fountain of rainbow light symbolises the reward for the labour of climbing the difficult path to the top.

30 Cormorant
The bird stands on a rock at the waterside, and looks at an illuminated passage between two huge candles, leading to 'the Light'. The passage is edged with a rainbow as a border between the darkness and the light. Above is the violet flame of transmutation.

31 Crane
In the sky is a celestial body showing a yin/yang design, symbol of the loving balancing of opposing forces that have to be united. The river can be walked through, because some rocks in the water connect the landscapes, so they are not really divided. The rainbow is protecting a high pillar, where the bright radiating light shows the unification of all colours.

32 Hummingbird
The hummingbirds rise on the soundwaves of the 'eternal OM', the OM of existence, made visible as the OM-symbols in the background.

33 Sunbird
The radiant sunbirds are sitting on the edges of their own 'suns', which have sunbird silhouettes within them (companionship). There are rainbow ribbons (joy), jewels (material gifts), and the universe (spiritual gifts) completing the rest of the picture.

34 Vulture
The vulture sits on a 'floating rock' as the symbol for something that
needs forgiveness. Hidden deep inside the rock is a bowl with a light,
symbolic of the light and love of Self, that sometimes is hidden in
the deepest corners. (While I was doing the hummingbirds over and
over again – five times without feeling satisfied – suddenly the vulture
announced itself, and after finishing the vulture, I could complete the
hummingbirds without any problem.)

35 Pheasant
The majestically beautiful, shining pheasant was in my garden often, as
he is every year, but he had never been as magnificent as the year I was
drawing this card. I took many photographs of him; he was made of
such an array of glorious colours…I was speechless with admiration. So
I put him on a pedestal, with radiating circles of light around him.

36 Turkey
The illuminated stairs, covered with jewels, symbolise the wonderful
help that has been received to reach this place.

37 Lovebird
In a green jewel-heart with crystal facets, a second lovebird is seen
(actually it is my own lovebird – he has been sitting on my head and
shoulders during the whole process of drawing the cards, so I wanted
to give him a place, too). In the opened heart, the universe is visible.
Green is the colour of the heart chakra, yellow is the colour of wisdom.
In the sky two illumined hearts are seen – in one of them Archangel
Michael is visible. (This Michael silhouette appeared while I was
drawing, I did not do this consciously; this was really amazing for me
– I have not used a 'human' form in any of the cards.) The yellow bow of
light is the forcefield of love.

38 Phoenix

The phoenix is still holding onto a branch of the past, a reality which is falling apart and burning, and behind the falling puzzle-pieces appears a peaceful world, full of promises for a new life filled with joy and light. (The idea of the puzzle-pieces falling apart suddenly came to my mind during the pause of a concert that a good friend had invited me to go to with her. I wrote it down, not knowing at the time which bird I should use it for.)

39 Cuckoo

This card I felt I had to do immediately after the roller (see note with 'the Roller'). As a sign of a new beginning, I made the buddhistic Wheel of Time radiating in the tree, and the tree itself shows the whole cycle of the seasons – buds, green leaves, brown leaves and dead leaves falling. In the background the trees are in spring-summer-autumn-winter, too.

40 Warbler

The beautiful song of the warbler connects and balances the radiant symbols of the heart chakra (green) and of the throat chakra (blue), which then makes it possible for the crown chakra to open completely (the golden one in the centre). The three chakras together sing of love and spiritual fulfilment.

41 Roller

I was drawing the roller on 11 September, 2001, when the destruction of the twin towers of the World Trade Centre in New York occurred. I had just finished the bird, and had only to do the feet and the background. It felt as though it was deeply symbolic to be drawing this bird at that moment – that the world had the possibility to make a choice at that time to shift from separation into Oneness. Below the bird the 'new' light is visible, shining behind what seems like a separation, covered with clouds (illusion). Above the bird is a symbolic representation of the reacquaintance of Self with God – where they meet, a bright light shines.

42 Oriole
The radiant yellow colour of the oriole gives warmth and joy when one is tired. It is sitting on a large cluster of citrine crystals (protection coming from within, and life-force). On the right side, under the sun, is a field of abundantly-flowering sunflowers. On the left side the flowers look dead and brown, because the sunforce energy has left.

43 Weaver
There is a landscape with all sorts of 'homes'; a home in this world, a home in a different world (other planets), a group of birds as a symbol of the 'family' of which one is part.

44 Partridge
For this card I did not really have anything in mind; the only thing I knew was that I had to make a high horizon, so that the bird could be really 'grounded'. So I placed the horizontal line, and the rest just happened. The partridge is in a circle of rose-quartz (love), with a rainbow sky in the background as a symbol of God's love. The candle is there as a guiding light to draw one's attention to the Divine Love.

45 Wagtail
To be happy the wagtail drinks from a fountain of light, coming from a 'sunstone' (joy and vitality). A rain of flowers comes from a rainbow bowl.

46 Raven
This was also a special card to illustrate. I drew the first attempt, and after having the idea of the universe pulled aside by the raven, I tried ways to make God visible, which was of course impossible. So I made a new card in which the raven raises the veils behind which, beyond the universe, God is found, the real goal of life. Here there is no separation.

47 Gannet
The gannet sits amongst the many gifts and treasures that are symbolic of the blessings that life is offering to be enjoyed, if one gives oneself permission to receive. A pearl moon radiates abundance over the earth. In the cave shines a light with the promise of more gifts to be explored.

48 Shrike

As a symbol for anger, the sword has cleaved the rock in two – this makes visible the lighted cross (Love), which is breaking through the clouds that might obscure it. The shrike sits on a 'crown of thorns', also reminding us of the power and love of the Christ energy that is available to each of us when we stand in our own truth.

49 Wren

The golden 'branch' on which the wren sits is the golden road (insight). On the light side of the road is abundance, prosperity, love. There are rock crystals in the upper landscape (balance, clarity). Below the golden road it is sombre, symbolising negativity, subconscious beliefs. Here there is smokey quartz (cleansing of negativity, transformation and stability). The landscape is actually one, only the thoughts that are chosen determine whether the experience is light or dark.

50 Ostrich

The ostrich is looking with a very conscious expression at its own lightbody, the light it really is.

51 Nightjar

The nightjar is a night bird, which lives (symbolically) in deep, dark caves. If it dares to follow the stairs that lead to the light of the inner self, it will discover that there are no fears left (the huge space of the universe, filled with beautiful stars and a moon).

52 Woodpecker

After the hard work to make the hole in the tree, the real goal will become visible at the right place and timing. Other efforts sometimes have no results (the other tree), but that is no reason to give up.
The castle with the difficult road is there as another reminder of the perseverance needed to arrive at the goal

53 Rooster

This one just happened. I started with the bird, and the rest created itself (and speaks for itself!)

54 Dodo

For the dodo, I felt very strongly that I should use 'snowflake obsidian' (for consciously releasing old emotions and blockages). So I made a gate that the dodo should go through to step out of a world where everything is extinguished, old and no longer alive.

Some time after doing this drawing, I discovered in one of my books that the dodo only lived on two volcanic islands – this was completely new to me, and I was amazed, considering the strong feeling that I had had to choose a volcanic mineral (obsidian) for this bird.

55 Blue Bird of Happiness

This symbolic bird totally created itself while I was drawing it, as did the background. I cannot say much about it, only that there is an atmosphere of real happiness with all those rainbow colours, and the bright shining sun.

Index